Vietnam Combat

An Attack Pilot's Diary

The Four Freedoms Betrayed

Captain David E. Leue' USN (Ret)

About the author

Captain David Leue' joined the Navy while a senior at Buffalo Technical High School. In his thirty-two year naval career he moved through the ranks from Apprentice Seaman to Captain. As a fighter/attack pilot he survived 329 combat missions flying from the decks of the aircraft carriers USS Boxer, USS Valley Forge, USS Philippine Sea, USS Coral Sea and USS Constellation, fighting for freedom in Korea and Vietnam.

Significant commands were: Commander Carrier Air Wing Seven; Squadron Commander Attack Squadron One Fifty-Three; Captain of USS Canisteo AO-99, a 650 foot armed replenishment ship; Chief of Staff Carrier Group Three; and Chief of Staff, Light Attack Wing, Pacific at NAS Lemoore, California.

His education includes the Armed Forces Staff College, a Bachelor of Science in Physics from the University of California at Berkeley and a Master's of Science in Engineering/Industrial Technology, California State University, Fresno, emphasizing solar energy.

Following naval service, he established Leue' Solar Inc., designing and installing many unique solar systems in the San Joaquin Valley. He then served as Professor of Engineering/Construction Management, California State University Fresno followed by twenty years as an Engineer with Pacific Gas & Electric working on energy efficiency projects in the food and agriculture industry.

He flies his own aircraft and lives with his wife, Stella, in Clovis, California.

CONTENTS

Vietnam Combat

Dedication

This book is dedicated to my Attack Squadron One Fifty-Three shipmates who gave their lives in the cause of freedom for the Vietnamese and Southeast Asian people.

Acknowledgments

The mentoring, critiques and encouragement of Janice Stevens and her Writers for Publication Group in Clovis, California were key in developing the skills and techniques necessary for the completion of this book. The professional editing and guidance of my wife, Stella and our daughter, Rebecca Roth were critical to the book's high quality. The excellent photos provided by my VA-153 shipmate, O.J. Greene, greatly enhanced the manuscript. The assistance of Peter Fokos facilitated the smooth compilation of the required computer inputs for publication. To all, my heartfelt thanks.

Preface

"Cannon to the right of them.

Cannon to the left of them.

Cannon in front of them.

Volley and thunder.

Storm'd at with shot and shell.

Boldly they rode and well.

Into the jaws of death.

Into the mouth of hell.

Rode the six hundred "

From the Charge of the Light Brigade by Alfred, Lord Tennyson

The terrors faced by the British Light Brigade in their failed 1854 Battle of Balaclava and Navy carrier squadrons fighting in Vietnam, were strikingly similar. Both faced Russia as an adversary. Both entered battle with great courage and flawed strategies. Both were pawns in larger political battles. Both paid a very dear price.

There, the similarity ends. The Light Brigade fought but a single battle. Navy squadrons fought for ten years. British poets memorialized their warriors. American poets distorted and diminished their warriors sacrifice.

I am old enough to have witnessed our government's total support of our WWII ally, Stalin. Kept from me and the nation, were Stalin's atrocities, his blood purges of his own Bolshevik party, his plan for world domination. Later it was explained, "Support of Stalin was for a good cause, we did it to defeat

Hitler." Yet, when Stalin's successors became our enemy, first in Korea, then in Vietnam, these same American government elites and pundits systematically destroyed the reputations of our friends in the minds of the American people.

In 1963, South Vietnamese President Diem, a life-long patriot, who fought for his people against the French, Japanese and the Communist, was vilified, then killed by President Kennedy!

Similarly, in 1973, President Thieu, was repeatedly attacked by our government and press. Apparently, these non-Communist patriots did not meet the far left standards set by our government élites. They were dealt with appropriately. At the same time, the crimes of our enemy, Ho Chi Minh, who allowed no freedoms and annihilated all opposition, were studiously ignored. Ask yourself, why?

In researching over thirty post conflict histories of the Vietnam conflict, I am struck by the irony that many of these tomes were penned by former press members who tacitly supported our enemies. In Naval Air, we have a term, "Covering your six." What these authors wrote is probably not good history. I will try to add some balance.

The fight for Vietnam was part of the continuing battle for freedom and justice in the world.

My perspective of Vietnam, set forth in this volume, reflects forty years studying history, enlightened by over three hundred combat missions flown in Korea and Vietnam.

David Leue'

Captain USN

CHAPTER ONE

A Fighter Pilot in the Future?

The Summer of 1943.

It was a very hot summer. My mother, sister Dolly, and I were living at 80 Virgil Avenue, the tough side of Buffalo, New York. Summertime, humid with no air-conditioning, crowded into an upper flat, next to hundreds of others.

Mother, bless her, had friends high up in the Lutheran Church. My grandfather had been a prominent Lutheran minister before he passed away. Mother, through her connections in the church, arranged for Dolly and I to go to camp Lutherland in the Pocono Mountains of Pennsylvania! That's what well-to-do families did with their kids in the summer, those days. However, we were not well-to-do, we would go to camp, not as paying members, but as workers. We could participate in camp activities as work permitted. We were both ecstatic. Dolly was a stunningly beautiful eighteen year old, I was a skinny fifteen.

Of course, Dolly got the only suitcase in the family. My suitcase was the so-called "Polish Suitcase," a bedspread tied together at the four corners. Dolly doesn't remember this, but I could never forget my embarrassment.

We started out by trolley from our corner on Virgil Avenue, to the train station downtown, where we boarded a marvelous steam train which travelled through western New York, and on to Lutherland. This trip took about five or six hours.

When we arrived, Dolly was assigned as lifeguard at the main facility, I was sent to the boy's camp, Camp Chickagami, situated on the far side of a large lake. It had rustic wood cabins around a central dining hall. Each cabin held six to eight boys, ages 14 to 16. The cabins were open with mosquito netting around the sides that was replaced every year. The dining area was open on all sides with a raised wood floor and a covered wood roof held up by log poles.

I was assigned as dishwasher and waiter. I set tables, served, cleared tables, washed dishes, with three or four boys from Pennsylvania.   They called themselves Pennsylvania Dutch, but were really of German extraction and spoke with an accent. They were good, rough, country boys. One played the old piano in the dining hall in off hours. We set tables, cleared tables and washed dishes for 200 boys and counselors three times a day.

The dishwasher was manual, it had a big mesh container that we filled with dishes, then pushed the big handle back and forth through soapy water twenty to thirty times each load. After that, the mesh basket was removed and placed into another tub to be rinsed. We dried the dishes by hand. It was hard work. We were not overly gentle and broke our share, which we promptly threw into the weeds in back of the open shed where we worked.

Work was hard. We had little time off. The Pennsylvania boys complained constantly. Apparently it was the first time they were away from home. The next thing I knew they all quit and went home. I was so naïve, I didn't complain, I just kept working by myself. I worked from the time I got up in the morning until I fell into bed at night. I did the whole thing and I really didn't know how to complain. Since everything was getting done, no one noticed. Finally, I said to myself, "I can't do this anymore!" I walked for about an hour to the other side of the lake, found Dolly and told her I was going home.

Dolly said I couldn't go home. Our return tickets were only good in three more weeks, besides she was having the time of her life as a beautiful eighteen year old life guard with hundreds of young WWII soldiers in the vicinity. So, she went directly to the top, and visited the Camp Director. The next thing I knew, they hired three new boys and I was in a favored position, doing just the silverware three times a day.

Now, I could do my job and participate in the swimming, boating hiking and other activities of the camp. I was having a great time. I got to know the others in my cabin, mostly New York City boys, tough, but good hearted and fun loving. I fit right in. Now, I had the time to swim, kayak or canoe and do many other activities. Too many.

The camp had a curfew at 9 PM; a counselor would come and check our beds. It did not take us long to figure out to wait until after bed check and then go out.

We did dumb things like set fire to the mosquito netting on other cabins. Someone told on us and we had some privileges taken away. We were gaining a reputation; we called ourselves, "The Instigators." It sounded bad. Of course, being fifteen and sixteen we talked incessantly of girls. We were strictly segregated from the girl's camp across the lake, except for very limited social events; however we would see the girls to talk and wave while boating.

My cabin mate, John, a New York City boy, a year older than myself, met a girlfriend from the girl's camp across the lake. At a planned get-together he introduced me to her pretty blond girlfriend, Patty, from Harrisburg, Pennsylvania.

This would never happened to me in Buffalo, I went to an all boys high school, was too shy, but now emboldened by my new independence, I was actually able to converse with a woman and act like a young man. At first, Patty and I would meet at the planned camp affairs. John, being from New York City, and wise in the ways of the world, would instruct me on the side. "Pay more attention to her, don't talk about yourself, women need lots of attention." What good advice!

It didn't take long for us to suggest meeting after bed check.

John and I would dress in our best slacks, walk the two miles to the other side of the lake and meet the girls. If a car came along, we would dive into the roadside brush and trees.

Sometimes, John and his girl, Patty and I, would tempt fate and go into the local malt shop together acting as old as we could hoping no one would turn us in. At other times we would sit and talk, walk in the woods, hug and kiss.

It was amazing that a beautiful real live woman thought I was something, and vice versa. The rules of behavior of young men and women in those days were quite clear and these trysts were quite innocent. Young ladies were under "threat of death" from their mothers. In most cases, exploring the wonders of women could only progress so far. Thank God. This was an amazing introduction for me to romance, with no harm done. As a male, it did wonders for my ego

Someone in my cabin, "The Instigators," maybe me, decided that it would be a really great stunt to take the diving board from the girl's camp swimming float in the middle of the night. We obtained several large wrenches from the tool shed and hid them in the bushes. That night, after bed check, four of us rowed quietly across the lake. In the dark, we patiently and quietly loosened the bolts, the board broke loose suddenly making a racket, lifting the boy with the wrench, and almost throwing him in the water. No lights went on in the girl's camp, we breathed a sigh of relief, then floated the board behind our boat and towed it to our side of the lake, where we hid it in the bushes.

The next morning, I was serving breakfast when I saw two rowboats filled with tough girl counselors coming across the lake. They pulled their boats up on the shore and came straight to our counselors. After a brief discussion, our camp's head counselor rounded up everyone from our cabin, "The Instigators." Since we had been in several scrapes before, they knew where to come. We were taken into a room and interrogated. When we were not forthcoming with any reasonable answers, they slapped us around and we confessed!

They fired me, and said I had to go home. I packed my things, then walked the long trip around the lake to tell Dolly I was fired. She once again went to the Camp Director, who got me reinstated and I went back to work.

Well, after that, I was really under a dark cloud. In fact, they watched us every night, and the late-night trips to see Patty had to cease. This is when they discovered the broken dishes out in back of the dishwasher.

It was during this period of time, I was feeling quite low and sorry for myself, and I took a rowboat out in the lake by myself. It was a beautiful sunny day, and although melancholy, I was enjoying the beauty of the lake, the mountains and the tranquility of the day.

The calm of this beautiful scene was shattered by the blast and roar of an Army Air Corps B-26, going flat out flying low on the water. The noise was terrific. He was buzzing his girlfriend, I assume, an activity that was indulged, due to the war. He pulled up sharply, turned around and made an even lower pass right over my boat. It brought tears to my eyes. I was thrilled and overwhelmed that anyone could do such a thing. The power, the skill, the freedom, the adventure, just went to the core of me. I said a fervent prayer from the heart. "Please God, let me fly someday, and please, please, let me do it well."

It was a prayer that would be answered.

The remainder of the time at Camp Chicagami was less stressful but enjoyable. I stayed out of trouble, met Patty on occasion. Fought a small forest fire that broke out near the camp, went boating and swimming. When the time came to depart it was sad. I saw Patty one more time the day I left. I hid my Polish Suitcase from her view. We talked about coming back again and promised to write.

Patty and I wrote to each other for about a year after I went back to Buffalo. We both went on with or lives, I often wondered about Patty and what her life was like. She was a sweet girl.

The summer of 1943. A great summer.

Be careful what you pray for.

CHAPTER TWO

Between Wars

1953-1963

The years between the battles in Korea with Fighter Squadron 24, described in Volume One, "Korean Combat," and the battles still to come in Vietnam, flew by. Life was good. During these years I was at home for significant periods of time. Our family prospered. Jane, a terrific Catholic woman, and I, now had five thriving daughters and a brand new son! Jane and the family knew only Navy life. They had adapted to its routines, challenges and benefits.

Emily, Cathy, Krista, Rebecca, Deborah, Paul and Jane Leue' Norfolk, 1962

I served in a series of interesting flying and staff billets. My first shore duty was flying in the Regulus Missile Program at the Naval Air Missile Test Center, Point Mugu, California, then later in Chincoteague, Virginia as part of the introduction of the Regulus cruise missile to the fleet. This tour included a deployment to the Mediterranean on USS Randolph. I flew a series of the latest jet fighters, including the F9F-6 Cougar, F2H Banshee and the FJ-3 Fury. Two years at the University of California at Berkeley followed. Here, I obtained a Bachelor's degree in Physics. Next came two years on the staff of Commander Naval Air Force US Atlantic Fleet in Norfolk, Virginia as Assistant for Guided Missile Training and Readiness.

Professionally, I had grown by serving in fleet squadrons and a major Fleet staff. My flying skills had developed significantly flying a series of the latest Navy jet fighters.

Orders to the Fleet

March 1962.

After my tour on the Commander in Chief US Atlantic Fleet Staff, I received orders to Light Attack Squadron Eighty One (VA-81), Carrier Air Wing Eight (CVW-8), attached to the USS Forrestal.

These orders to a fleet jet attack squadron, were exciting news. My squadron, VA-81, and USS Forrestal, were home ported at Naval Air Station, Oceana and Norfolk respectively. The family would not have to move! A first for us.

We were happy in our Meadowbrook Forrest, Norfolk rental home, however, with the recent arrival of son, Paul, we were now a family of eight. Jane and I began to look for a larger home. My smart-mouthed Protestant buddies joked, "Leue', look what you've done, you don't even have a place at the table."

Inquiries, revealed that my new squadron, VA-81, would deploy with USS Forrestal in August, 1962 for an extended Mediterranean cruise; therefore, Jane and I delayed our search for a new home until I returned from the upcoming eight-month cruise.

New Navy

I was very happy to be going back to a fleet jet squadron on several levels. First, I loved to fly; second, I fit best with operational people, they were doers and risk takers; third, this was the best career path. Naval Aviation had changed dramatically since my Korean war days. The Navy had reorganized carrier air wings into two fighter squadrons, two light attack squadrons, a propeller attack squadron and one heavy attack squadron.

The revolutionary change, however, was in training with the institution of the Replacement Air Group concept. Under this new concept, all pilots and crewmen with orders to a fleet squadron had to go through the Replacement Air Group (RAG), and be thoroughly and professionally re-trained in the new aircraft. This training included: safety, instruments, familiarization, formation, tactics, night flying, bombing, rockets, strafing, nuclear delivery, night and day carrier qualification.

My orders were to VA-43 the A4 Skyhawk RAG at Oceana, Virginia. My first course was instrument training then a complete ground school covering all of the A4 Skyhawk systems. The training proceeded on the various phases mentioned above. Only after completing this six month syllabus, would I join Attack Squadron 81. This so-called RAG training greatly improved Fleet standardization, professionalism and safety. Fleet accident rates dropped dramatically. This training enabled all Navy squadrons to fly from carriers both night and day, all over the world. A dramatic change from my Korean War days, when only special-teams flew at night.

The Replacement Air Group Squadron (RAG), VA-43

I breezed through the RAG training. I quickly came to feel at home and even admire the A4 Skyhawk. It was designed by Ed Heinemann, the famous Douglas Aircraft chief designer. It was originally conceived as a simple, lightweight, fast, nuclear delivery aircraft. It was amazingly agile and compact. The cockpit was only an inch or two wider than my shoulders, it fit me perfectly. Early in its development, it had set speed records. It had a very good range and proved to be an excellent all-around attack aircraft.

VA-43 A4B Skyhawk

It was very maneuverable, a fine fighter in its own right. It was fun to fly, amazingly strong, honest, with no bad habits. However, the early model we flew, the A4D-2, renamed the A4B, was a marginal night carrier airplane. It had no autopilot, with only a very small attitude gyro and no radar. Cockpit lighting left much to be desired. Night carrier work in the A4B would prove to be one of the biggest challenges of my flying career.

Ron "Gunga" Dinn, Captain USAF

I met Air Force exchange Captain Ron Dinn, USAF going through VA-43. Of course, everyone called him "Gunga" Dinn. The Air Force, to foster inter-service understanding, detailed some of their best officers on exchange duty with the Navy. Captain Gunga Dinn

Capt Ron Dinn, USAF

was one of these outstanding officers. He was headed for VA-81 as I was, and we became fast friends. Ron and I qualified in night carrier landings on the USS Enterprise July 17, 1962. The weather at Oceana was below minimums when we completed our night qualifications. We were vectored to Marine Corps Air Station, Cherry Point, where I shot an actual Ground Controlled Approach (GCA), with Gunga Dinn on my wing. This completed our RAG training. We joined Attack Squadron 81 shortly thereafter and deployed with Carrier Air Wing Eight onboard USS Forrestal to the Mediterranean for an eight month cruise on August 1, 1962.

Attack Squadron Eighty One (VA-81)

Attack Squadron 81's Commanding Officer was Commander Nick Longfield, the Executive Officer was Commander Grover Gregory, the Operations officer was Lieutenant Commander Jerry Brummitt, the Maintenance Officer was Lieutenant Commander Fred Whittemore and the Administrative Officer was Lieutenant Jerry Tappan. I was assigned the duties of Assistant Operations and Training Officer. Gunga Dinn was given the job of Flight Officer.

I could tell immediately that VA-81 was a happy, professional squadron. This was a fine group of dedicated officers. I was to find we had equally professional and dedicated enlisted with outstanding Chief Petty Officers.

Light Attack Squadron Eighty One VA-81, USS Forrestal

Although I was new to the A4 Skyhawk, I fit easily into the squadron routine. I found I was the only officer in the squadron with combat experience. The tempo of this Mediterranean cruise was not that of peacetime, it was intense. We were in the Mediterranean as a counterforce to the Russians. All pilots had been trained in the delivery of nuclear weapons. We all had targets in the Soviet Union or its satellites. This was our primary mission; we practiced our skills night and day.

From the perspective of 50 years, this period of time is amazingly clear. Forrestal was the first of the new class of larger carriers. She had four steam catapults, angled deck and the Fresnel landing system. These changes, pioneered by the British, significantly increased the ship and air wing capabilities as well as safety. However, the Navy was experimenting with very low levels of flight deck lighting. This combined with the lack of night features in the A4B made night carrier landings during this period especially challenging, indeed terrifying. I recall the great anxiety of getting back aboard Forrestal in one piece during black Mediterranean nights.

However, my confidence and skills continually improved throughout the cruise as I adapted to the A4B's deficiencies. I felt reasonably competent at night by the end of the cruise. I didn't know it at the time, but this experience would help keep me alive in the combat to come in Vietnam.

Vietnam Combat on the Horizon

We were anchored off Naples, Italy, I had the duty. I was reading the newspaper's Sunday Supplement. There was a long article on Ngo Dinh Diem, the President of South Vietnam. It was very negative. Typically the article said nothing about the threat from the Communist Ho Chi Minh and his Soviet supported regime in North Vietnam where there were absolutely no freedoms.

It was January 1963.

Having fought in Korea with the same dynamics, I was super sensitive to the Communist threat in Vietnam. Out loud, I said, "Here we go again, the press and government are bad-mouthing our friends. You can bet that we will be at war in South Vietnam within the next couple of years." A near-by squadron mate spoke up, dismissing my analysis summarily. He said, "Leue' you don't know what you are talking about."

Left: Catapulting F4 Phantoms   Right: Catapulting an A3D Skywarrior

Unfortunately, my fears became a reality in not too many months. In May 1963, the papers reported South Vietnam President Diem had been assassinated during an attempt by President Kennedy to liberalize the South Vietnamese regime! Now South Vietnam had no leader and Ho Chi Minh got an unexpected boost in his attempt to overthrow and take over South Vietnam.

We had no idea at the time, but Lieutenant Commanders Fred Whittemore, Jerry Tappan, Charlie Hunter and I, would all end up in Vietnam before too long.

Change of Command

Midway through the cruise Commander Bob Gore took over from Commander Nick Longfield as Commanding Officer of VA-81. Commander Grover Gregory remained as Executive Officer. This was unusual, normally the Executive Officer of a squadron is promoted to Commanding Officer.

A VA-81 Skyhawk launches from Forrestal's waist steam catapult

Cold War Operations

I began the cruise with 230 carrier landings, only seven of them at night. This cruise would greatly increase my night carrier experience and confidence. Getting that experience was not easy. My logbook shows that during this Mediterranean cruise I made

96 carrier landings, 27 at night. Night landings at the end of the cruise were still a challenge, but I felt much more confident. This was a formative time for modern naval aviation in general, as it adapted to flying high performance aircraft night and day from carriers in all weather.

During this period of time, there were two carrier task groups in the Mediterranean. These carrier forces, with the deployed ballistic missile submarines and the Air Force long-range bombers, constituted the Triad of nuclear forces facing the Soviet Union.

Our morale was high, we believed in our mission. We paid a price. Although this was technically peace time, each time we went to sea we lost shipmates. First, an F8 pilot was killed when the catapult bridal came off his aircraft during launch and he crashed into the sea. Next, on a stormy night, an A3 Sky Warrior made several passes at the deck, but could not get aboard, so he was vectored to Sardinia. This A3 disappeared forever with a crew of three.

Later, the Commanding Officer of our AD Skyraider squadron, was killed when he stalled and spun his aircraft while executing a weapons delivery maneuver. VA-81, lost Lieutenant Junior Grade Larry Staples at night, when he flew into the water on his approach to the ship. Later, Lieutenant Junior Grade J. Blanke of VA-83, flew into the water and was killed when dive bombing the spar aft of the ship. Then, Lieutenant Junior Grade Paul Norton of VA-81, flamed out, bailed out at night, but was rescued; thanks to the good work of his Section Leader, Lieutenant Commander Fred Whittemore. Air Wing 8 lost seven pilots and eight aircraft, all on a so-called, "peacetime cruise" to the Mediterranean.

Flying off the ship over the ocean at night is 100% instruments. There was very rarely any horizon. Our night missions were scheduled to practice various skills, such as in-flight refueling, navigation, instruments, bombing, and of course, night carrier landings.

The typical night launch would involve 10 to 20 aircraft. To recover these aircraft in an orderly manner we were assigned a holding point called, "Marshall." The lowest Marshall point was usually 20,000 feet 20 miles aft of the ship on the reciprocal of the expected recovery heading. Forrestal practiced what we called, "Zip Lip", which meant, except in emergencies, we did not use the radio. Flights were expected to go to their assigned Marshall point in time to push over at the assigned Expected Approach Time, (EAT). In flights of two, the leader pushed over at his Expected Approach Time, then the wingmen did a 360° orbit to push over two minutes later.

After pushing over from Marshall, we put out our speed brakes, power back to 80%, descending at 250 knots and 5000 feet per minute until reaching 5000 feet. We called this, "Platform," then we reduced our decent rate to 1000 feet/minute, leveling at 600 feet at 3 miles aft of the ship.

Landing gear and flaps were lowered. At a mile and a half aft of the ship, the ship's runway lights dimly came into view, followed by the Fresnel lens, and the center line lights.

Early in the cruise, at this point, I would get a severe case of vertigo: the ship's runway lights would appear to be floating below me. It took all my will power not to drop my nose and stay on glide slope, holding the orange ball in the center of the green datum, correcting right or left to stay on the centerline and holding a "doughnut" on my angle of attack indicator.

In close, the ship appeared to rush at me out of the blackness with increasing velocity... until Bam! I flew into the deck with a satisfying jolt. Full throttle, I'm thrown up into the straps, my face an inch or two from the gun sight.

It felt great. I was home.

Off with the throttle, hook up, lights out, hit the left brake as I rolled back, the nose rotates to the right, power on to cross the foul line and clear the landing area for my wingman. Bam! My wingmen arrests to my left. I taxi up to the bow, crewmen tie me down, I go below and de-brief with my wingman and the Landing Signal Officer (LSO). He grades all of our approaches. "Okay Three Wire" is the best. It felt good to be aboard and alive.

Mediterranean Liberty

The ship's routine was to operate extensively night and day for three weeks at sea and then spend four to seven days in a selected Mediterranean port. We visited such great places as Cannes, France; Beirut, Lebanon; Barcelona, Spain; Livorno, Italy; Naples, Italy; and Massena, Sicily to name a few.

The stress of months at sea, coupled with the ever present danger of carrier operations, led us to act as sailors immemorial. We tended to drink too much ashore. Gunga Dinn, my roommate, and I usually went on liberty together. He was a very hard drinking guy and it became my duty to get him back aboard in one piece. Jerry Tappan and Whit Whittemore were out of the same mold. They were all terrific officers, outstanding aviators, but sometimes collectively, they exhibited too much color on the beach.

The ship was scheduled to be in Cannes, France over Christmas 1962. (Another Christmas away from the family). The squadron officers pooled their resources and we rented a villa in Cannes. Cannes, France in the summertime is overrun with all the hoi-ploy of Europe, but in the winter it turned into a quiet French town. We would go ashore, buy fresh French bread and cheese and red wine at the local market, then retire to our villa with a book, or walk the beautiful streets and beaches.

I thought the villa in Cannes was just great, but it was too quiet for Jerry Tappan and Gunga Dinn. They had to go to Monaco to the Casino. After a few too many drinks, Gunga Dinn thought it would be funny to steal the casino fire ax off of the wall and bring it back to the squadron as a souvenir. Unfortunately, he was spotted and as he ran down the marble stairs to escape, he tripped, fell, was captured and put in jail. I had to go the next day and get him bailed out and promise that he wouldn't come back.

The second incident took place in Beirut, Lebanon in 1963. Beirut was a very peaceful and beautiful city. Gunga Dinn and I ended up in a Beirut pizza place at about midnight. We ordered a very unique pizza, it had a fried sunny side up egg on top. Gunga had too much to drink and was telling me a sad story about his early boyhood problems with his father. He became very emotional and he put out his cigarette in our pizza, ruining it. I got him started back down to the Fleet Landing. We left that great pizza mostly uneaten.

We took the one o'clock liberty boat back to the ship. I went down the passageway from our room to the Head to take a shower and then went to bed. I had the upper bunk in our room. I awoke with a start about 5 AM. I looked down and realized, Gunga was not in his bunk. I contemplated reporting this to the duty officer; he was in bad shape when we came aboard, maybe he fell over the side. I had visions of him hanging on the anchor chain yelling, "Help!" At about that time the hatch to our room opened and Gunga came in, very disheveled, still in his liberty clothes. I said, "Gunga, where have you been? I thought you fell over the side". He said, "Louie, I know how much you liked that pizza I ruined. I went ashore on the next boat and bought you a new one. I missed the last boat, I spent the night on the pier."

Now, that's a true friend, the type of guy you'd want with you when you went to war.

Fleet Landing in Cannes.   Capt Ron Dinn

During this period of time, Franco was in power in Spain. Of course he was a dictator and had a bad name in the U.S. Personally, I always felt he saved Spain and the Catholic Church from Communism. Franco's Spain in 1963 was a beautiful place especially compared to Italy, France or anywhere behind the Iron Curtain. None of this found its way into the U.S. press, which always portrayed Franco in a very negative light. The Left hated him and Franco was very hard on them, which was okay with me. On the plus side, Franco liked the U.S. military and the Spanish people loved the American military. Spain was the only country in Europe where we could go ashore in uniform. The people were delightful. They seemed free and happy to me. I liked Spain best of all the European countries we visited.

On one occasion, Gunga Dinn and I went on liberty in Barcelona, our favorite liberty port, in our dress blues. We had a great dinner at a very quaint restaurant in the older part of town called, "Los Caracoles," which means, The Snails. After dinner we went past a shop that was selling fine Spanish brandy, "Fundador," for only $.90 a liter. What a buy! We had taken a suitcase for souvenirs, so we filled it with brandy. On the way back to the Fleet Landing, we stopped at a local nightclub for a drink. They were dancing the new dance, the "Twist." The price of a dance with a local lovely was a drink. Spanish brandy was cheap, right?

Well, we danced the night away, figuring that the bill would be nothing to worry about. Of course, sailors all over the world, from the beginning of time, have fallen for that same trap. The bill took every single Spanish posada and American dollar that Gunga and I had in our pockets.

We went outside, Gunga said, "I'll hail a taxi." I said, "Gunga we don't have a cent, we will have to walk." It was about 5 miles to the Fleet Landing. Gunga said, "No way," and he hailed a taxi. We got in and he said, "I'll borrow the money from the Beach Guard." We rode to the Fleet Landing. When we arrived, I stood by the taxi as Gunga went over to ask the Beach Guard for some money. Gunga came back with a long look and said, "They wouldn't loan me any money." (No kidding, Dick Tracy!)

We stood there looking at each other and wondering what to do. The taxi driver glared at us, waiting for his money. In desperation, I thrust my hands deep down into the bottom of my Navy Bridge Coat pockets in frustration. One pocket had a rip, my hand went way down into the lining, I felt a bill! It was five posada note! (We called them "potatoes"). That paid our bill. I said a silent, "Thank You, Lord."

The first officer's motor boat pulled in with our squadron buddies, who had the duty on the ship that night. They were coming ashore to go on a tour. They razzed us for being gone all night and went on their way. Gunga Dinn and I stepped aboard the officer's motorboat and headed back to USS Forrestal. Once back aboard ship, we had a full day ahead of us. I was a Training Officer and I had published a schedule for the morning's training in the ready room starting at 0900. These training sessions covered topics such as: aviation safety, gunnery procedures, dive bombing techniques, squadron doctrine, fitness reports, schedules, port visits, the culture of Italy, Spain, France etc.

The Navy required that one third of the crew of any Navy ship be onboard while in port. This was a hold over from the disaster at Pearl Harbor. So, we spent a good share of our time aboard ship, even when in port. After my liberty with Gunga Dinn, having set up the training for the day, I went to the back of the ready room and fell asleep. After the training ended the squadron officers saw me asleep and everyone silently left the ready room, turned out the lights and locked the ready room hatch.

I woke up in a dark ready room, locked in. I didn't know where I was. Big joke.

March 1963.

Returning Home. After eight months, USS Forrestal and Carrier Air Wing Eight returned to the US. Jane and I had written almost every day but I had so much to catch up on. Son, Paul, who I had only known briefly before we deployed, was now over a year old.

It was great to see how Debbie, Krista, Cathy, Emily and Becky had grown and prospered. Jane had done a terrific job as usual, while I was gone and all were thriving. In real terms, what Jane did, raising the family, with love and devotion and dedication, was so

Becky, Debbie, Krista, Cathy, Emily, Jane & Paul

much greater than anything I had accomplished, half way around the world.

We had grown out of our rental house in Meadowbrook Forrest. Jane and I searched for and bought a new four-bedroom home in Virginia Beach. We put a fence around the yard, planted grass so the children would have a safe place to play.

Papa's Home! Leue's in front of new house Virginia Beach 1964

We traded in our vulnerable 1955 Ford station wagon for a used 1962 Chevrolet nine passenger station wagon with overdrive. We used this Chevrolet for trips to the John Kerr Dam on the Roanoke River in North Carolina. We would tow our boat filled with the camping gear and dog, Herbie.

We had good times camping and fishing and looking for Indian arrow heads. Later we branched out on trips to the Great Smoky Mountains National Park and a primitive campground at Cataluchi Creek. On our first trip to the Great Smokey

Mountains, North Carolina, we drove all night then pulled in to the campground at about 5 AM. As we were unloading gear, I put Paul in the front seat to keep him out of trouble. He leaned on the horn ring and announced to everyone that the Leue's had arrived.

We had many fun trips to the Smokey Mountains. I have 8mm footage of these affairs. Jane was a trooper and put up with changing diapers and wet sleeping bags in the often rainy weather of the Smoky 's.

On one of these trips, it was unusually rainy, Jane and I were standing in a downpour, we looked at each other and said together, "It's time to leave." Everything we had was wet, so we packed it into our boat that we had pulled on a trailer. I opened the drain in the back, so the water would run out. Dog Herbie was a mess, so I tied him in the front of the boat under a tarp and we took off. Herbie strongly objected to this treatment. As long as I was moving Herbie would stay down, but as soon as we stopped at a light, he would stick his head up and bark like crazy at the cars next to us. People in cars on each side of us looked at me with scorn for abusing my dog. Finally, I had to stop and bring the big, wet, smelly, Herbie into the back of the station wagon with the kids.

I think it was on this same trip, we had a blow-out on the trailer at one o'clock in the morning near Greensboro, North Carolina. I had AAA, so I unhitched the trailer, found a payphone and called AAA asking for assistance. They told me my insurance didn't cover trailers. I spent the next three hours finding a tire and then the tools required to break open the old rusty split rim wheels.

New Aircraft

In August 1963, the squadron received the new A4-E aircraft. The A4-E had an autopilot, radar, a large attitude gyro and a more powerful Pratt Whitney engine. This aircraft would be a much better night attack aircraft. The A4 E also climbed better and was more fuel efficient.

Commander Gore was an excellent commanding officer. He set the general policy and let the department heads run the squadron. Jerry Brummitt departed and I became the Operations Officer. I laid out the syllabus for training in the new A4-E. After we became familiar with the characteristics of this new model of Skyhawk, we emphasized weapons training.

We practiced dive bombing, rocket attacks, strafing and lay down or minimum altitude weapons delivery. In addition, we practiced our nuclear delivery techniques which involved a 500 knot low level run-in to the target with a four G pull-up going over-the-top into a half loop, rolling upright on top (a half Cuban eight), then diving and escaping on the reciprocal course.

Later, I scheduled the entire squadron for extensive night training. Commander Gregory, the XO, gave me some grief about this, but the CO wanted the night work and we proceeded. We came to work about an hour before sunset and flew through the night. Night weapons deliveries were practiced as well as in-flight refueling and radar navigation. This training became the basis for my night combat capabilities in Vietnam.

1964 World's Fair, New York, New York

In early 1964, there was a World's Fair in New York City. The USS Forrestal was invited to attend and we tied up to Pier 90,

USS Forrestal New York Worlds Fair, 1964

New York City. Jane arranged for babysitters and met me in New York. We had great fun for two or three days going to the World's Fair and seeing the sights in New York City. We met my Aunt Ann and Uncle Richard Hanser, who lived in New York City. We invited them for a tour of the USS Forrestal and dinner onboard. The dinner turned out to be New England boiled dinner, not too impressive, but I think they enjoyed seeing the ship. Richard, co-authored the famous series, "Victory at Sea," with Henry Salomon, and music by Richard Rodgers.

Richard and Ann Hanser

A funny incident took place when we left the ship after dinner. There was a bar on the pier, Aunt Ann suggested we stop for a drink. The place was packed and we sat down on a bench against the wall side by side, Richard, Ann, Jane and myself, right to left. On my left were two English sailors with a young lady between them, all were "three sheets to the wind." I was in my dress blues. The English sailor next to me saw the gold stripes on my sleeve through his drunken haze. He put his head down to within a few inches of my stripes scrutinizing them closely, then looked up at me and exclaimed in a loud voice, "Two and a half rounds, man! You've made your mark!" Everyone laughed. Both sailors went back to hugging the lucky girl.

Coast to Coast Non-Stop in the A4-E

The publications for the A4-E were still incomplete at this time. We had no clear numbers on the fuel efficiency of the new Pratt Whitney engine. I suggested to Commander Gore that we take four airplanes to the West Coast, two aircraft with two 300 gallon drop tanks and two aircraft with three 300 gallon drop tanks. I selected Lieutenants Jerry Tappan and Red Gray and Captain Ron Dinn for this trip. We flew a series of low-level flights across country to Naval Air Station Lemoore, California. We recorded fuel flows and times. On the return flight, Jerry Tappan and I would attempt to fly nonstop from Naval Air Station Lemoore, California to Naval Air Station Oceana Virginia, un-refueled. We flew individually to achieve the best possible fuel efficiency. In fact, Jerry Tappan, that rat, got up very early without waking me. He was airborne before me, and was the first A4 pilot to achieve the record of flying across the country, nonstop un-refueled. I landed about 20 minutes after him with a flight time of four hours and 45 minutes. The information we gained from these flights allowed us to know precisely the fuel specifics of the A4-E.

Change of Command

In the spring of 1964, Commander Gregory was finally scheduled to take over the squadron as commanding officer. Commander Nick Castruccio, who would be our new Executive Officer, was still going through training in the A4 replacement squadron, VA-43. In the interim, I was appointed as Acting Executive Officer. This was good training for me.

Commander Gregory informed me that he wanted to have a formal Change of Command ceremony, with the squadron passing in review. I tried to dissuade him, pointing out that sailors don't routinely march in parades or pass in review, it may not be pretty. Commander Gregory insisted that we would pass in review. I did the best I could to ensure the squadron looked good. I scheduled drill training, marching, use of swords and passing in review each day after flying. We had a good crew, but they just didn't take it seriously and I had to raise "Cain" to whip them into shape. I would fall-in the squadron, then review and practice the procedures we would follow in the Change of Command. We had a drummer that would beat cadence as we practiced our marching commands: column left, column right, left face, right face, etc. The officers were drilled in the manual of arms for swords. We actually started to look pretty good. I felt more confident that we would put on a good show. Gunga Dinn was assigned the role of narrator. Admiral Hyland, Commander Carrier Division Four was scheduled to be the speaker.

The day of the Change of Command dawned bright and clear, the whole ceremony proceeded as planned. We stood resplendent in our dress whites with swords, at Parade Rest as Commander Gore, then Commander Gregory and Admiral Hyland gave their remarks.

Commander Gregory, now the Commanding Officer, turned to me and gave the command, "Pass in Review!" I called, "Squadron attention!," then, "Right face", then, "Pass in Review!" The drum started and we marched off in good order, "Squadron, left turn!" I started the squadron toward the reviewing stand. At that time I heard Admiral Hyland's high-pitched voice calling, "Hold It, Hold It." I called, "Squadron halt," and I heard the chaplain praying, "Dear Lord please bless the new Commanding Officer...........". Commander Gregory had not heard Gunga Dinn say, "The Chaplain will now give the benediction". Some how, we stumbled through the remainder of the "Pass in Review," after the chaplain had blessed us.

After all of this I quipped, "We should re-write the Ceremonies Manual and include, "Pass in Benediction" as an approved ceremony. Sailors should not "Pass in Review."

The change of command party was at the Breezy Point Officers Club at Norfolk Naval Station. After a few drinks, I spotted a pair of large Navy wings on the wall and suggested to Gunga Dinn that we spirit them out of the club for our ready room in Oceana. He agreed. We wrapped the wings in tissue paper left over from the gifts for Commander Gore, then walked out of the door carrying the wings between us. Unfortunately, a day later the Naval

Investigating Service called me and indicated that they knew who had taken the wings from the officers club. We promptly returned them to Breezy Pont. Nice try.

Orders to Armed Forces Staff College

The squadron trained vigorously in preparation for the next Mediterranean cruise on USS Forrestal in the Summer of 1964. Commander Nick Castruccio came aboard and we became fast friends. We had a lot in common. He was a fine aviator, a good Catholic with a large family, just like the Leue's. He was an outstanding Naval Academy officer and I learned many things from him. We deployed with USS Forrestal to the Caribbean in the Spring of 1964. At this time, I received orders to Armed Forces Staff College in Norfolk. Therefore, I would not be deploying with the squadron to the Mediterranean later in the year. I was assigned as a Special Projects Officer and Jerry Tappan took over as Operations Officer.

My last task in the squadron was to prepare a tactics booklet for the squadron, setting out in detail the type of tactics, weapons and fusing used for attacking various types of targets, night and day, if the squadron were sent to Vietnam. I'm not sure what Jerry Tappan and Grover Gregory did with this document, but the research and study was invaluable to me in my next assignment.

Last Flight

July 7, 1964. It would be my last flight in Attack Squadron 81. I was turning over the reins of Operations Officer, to my buddy, Lieutenant Commander Jerry Tappan. I scheduled us together, I said, "Jerry I'll meet you at 20,000 feet over Oregon Inlet, North Carolina." I took off and climbed to 30,000 feet circled and waited. Jerry showed up at 25,000 feet. (We both cheated).

I dove down on him; the fight was on; full power, pulling, straining against the "Gs", over the top, buffeting on the edge of a stall, diving, zooming, high G barrel rolls, repeated scissors at minimum speed, flaps down, both with equal airplanes and skills. Jerry was an outstanding aviator and he made no mistakes. We fought to a draw. Low on fuel, we returned to NAS Oceana wing on wing.

It was sad for me to leave VA-81, a fine squadron, with good friends. The squadron would deploy again in late July to the Mediterranean on USS Forestall. Nick Castruccio would go on to be Commanding Officer of the squadron. Unfortunately, a year later his wingman was killed when he and Nick were involved in air combat maneuvering with their sister squadron aircraft.

This hassling, between squadrons, was done by most of us on a daily basis. Air Combat Maneuvering (ACM) was really an essential part of our training. However, this un-briefed incident ended Nick Castruccio's career. I'm sure he would have gone on to be an Admiral.

Jerry Tappan, Fred Whittemore and I would all go on to fight in Vietnam. Fred would die there. Gunga Dinn would die in an F-104 accident at Luke Air Force Base within the year. Jerry Tappan would go on to command an A7 squadron and eject from an A7 and be rescued.

As I left the squadron, I knew none of this and I was excited to be selected to attend the Armed Forces Staff College. I would shortly screen for command. This was a giant step in my career. Best of all, the family was healthy and they looked forward, as a good Navy family does, to the next duty station.

CHAPTER THREE

Preparing for Command

Armed Forces Staff College

After detaching from Attack Squadron 81 on USS Forrestal, I went directly to the Armed Forces staff College located in Norfolk, Virginia.

Orders to the Armed Forces staff College was a good indication that I may go further in the United States Navy. More good news, the Armed Forces Staff College was located in Norfolk. We would not have to move the family again.

The Armed Forces Staff College course of instruction was an outstanding, concentrated, primer for future combat leaders and senior officers. This course brought together selected middle grade, Army, Navy, Marine and Foreign officers in a military/academic environment, that encouraged the exchange of ideas and experiences concerning world events, military capabilities, organizations and future conflicts.

The Armed Forces Staff College became the most important school I would attend (Sorry, Berkeley). The course was very intense lasting a year. I gained invaluable contacts, information on the capabilities of my sister services, appreciation of the military staff system and valuable speaking skills in this brief period of time.

Organization and Speakers

The school organized us into seminars of a dozen students that included Army, Marine Corps, Navy and foreign officers. We were all pay grade O-4, that is Lieutenant Commander or Major. Mornings the entire class gathered in a large auditorium for speeches by top people in the State Department, Department of Defense, Army, Navy, Air Force, Marine Corps or in Industry.

Some of these speakers were fantastic. Others were frankly terrible. Just observing these speakers, I learned what I should or should not do as a speaker. The first obvious mistake was made by those reading a speech written for them, which they weren't

Armed Forces Staff College

passionate about or really didn't totally understand. These speakers put us to sleep. The other big mistake I noted was made by the few that tried to completely memorize their speech word for word. I felt very sorry for one Navy Captain, who had memorized his speech word for word, then in the middle of his address he froze, his mind went blank. He had to excuse himself.

The speakers which I enjoyed and taught me the most, kept me interested and motivated, all spoke with passion about their subject and looked directly at the audience using few notes. I said to myself, "I can do that on subjects I know and feel strongly about." I lost my fear of public speaking.

Thereafter, I developed a simple system in preparing for a speech: I studied the subject in detail, then using note paper in long hand, I wrote: 1. A simple opening line, 2. Listed key words or facts in sequence, 3. Wrote my closing line. After rehearsing my speech, I was confident I could make my points with my head up, looking at my audience and close with a strong statement.

Seminars

In the afternoons, our seminar group of twelve officers, a mixture of Army, Marine, Navy and foreign officers, were given a problem based on the morning lectures. We were allotted a certain period of

Armed Forces Staff College Seminar

time to do individual research and develop solutions for the problem. We then presented our views, accepted criticism and did likewise for the others. We then worked out joint solutions. We examined Vietnam in particular, because, already in early 1964, the open fighting had begun. This interplay between services expanded my knowledge of Army and Marine capabilities and greatly increased my respect for their professionalism and capabilities. I was particularly impressed with the Army officers, who generally had been to several Army staff schools before coming to The Armed Forces Staff College. I learned from the Marine and foreign officers as well. All of my classmates would fight in Vietnam.

Vietnam Heats Up

August 2, 1964. The destroyer USS Maddox, on patrol in the Gulf of Tonkin, off of Vihn, Vietnam, was attacked by three North Vietnamese Torpedo Boats. These PTs were driven off and damaged by the Maddox's five and three inch gunfire and by Navy F8 fighters from the USS Ticonderoga.

On August 4th the destroyers Maddox and Turner-Joy were again attacked by PTs. Congress subsequently passed the "Tonkin Gulf Resolution." authorizing strikes against Vietnam. The second attack, which occurred at night, has been wrapped in controversy ever since. Unfortunately, this incident masks the real origin of the conflict in Vietnam, the silent invasion of South Vietnam by Communist forces from the north, which began years before.

Thesis

We were required to write a thesis on a selected pertinent subject. I chose the mistreatment of our prisoners in Korea. A recent book by an obvious left-wing writer, Thomas Kincaid, "In Every War but One," had greatly provoked me.

Kincaid's book was condensed and published in the New Yorker magazine. Kincaid's thesis was: during the Korean War, the reason 58% of Americans died in North Korean and Chinese prisons was, they were poorly trained and disciplined. (He concluded, it was our fault.)

I read every book on the subject I could find and wrote my thesis based on this research. I came to the conclusion that Kincaid's premise was not only incorrect, it was based on a very anti-US bias. Many books refuted Kincaid's arguments, but "March to Calumny" by Biederman was the most powerful. Biederman documented: In World War II, 66% of Americans in died in Japanese prisons, while only 3% died in German prison camps! In other words, American prisoners under the Japanese died at a rate TWENTY TIMES those captured by the Germans, all with the same training and discipline. Biederman proved, the key factor in prisoner survival, is prisoner treatment. (No kidding!). None of this ever got any notice by the US Press. You might ask: Why isn't this wide gap in the treatment of American WW II prisoners in Japan and Germany common knowledge in this country?

I felt good about my research, the logic of my thesis, and I received an excellent grade, even if the paper was not well structured with many minor errors.

However, my conclusions were terribly prophetic, I concluded:

1. The Communist in Korea had grossly abused prisoners, by starving and torturing to extort false statements for propaganda and political gain.

2. Unless these facts were made known to the world, the Communist would use these methods in future conflicts in Vietnam or Cuba.

I recommended that we go to the United Nations immediately, with evidence from our returning prisoners and expose the horror of the Communist technique of using torture for political gain. If we did not, the Communist would surely use these methods effectively against us in the next conflict, either in Cuba or Vietnam.

Too soon, my predictions were to come true. In Vietnam, the North Vietnamese would torture, in some cases to death, American prisoners, many my friends, to extort propaganda and hold them as hostages, which influenced an early withdrawal and defeat.

Promotion and Selection for Command

Just before graduation at the Armed Forces Staff College, I

Promotion to Commander, June 1965

received the very good news that I had been promoted to Commander and screened for command of Attack Squadron 153, attached to USS Coral Sea in the Pacific Fleet. This was a major career milestone and it meant that I would certainly be involved directly in the Vietnam conflict.

Jane was not pleased with my assignment to a squadron already deployed to South East Asia, but she supported me in my career

Leue's heading west, Humphries Peak   Leue's at the Grand Canyon

and we both eagerly looked forward to the adventure of a new duty station. She was the best of Navy wives.

Based on my experience in Korea I strongly believed that, with the proper national policies and application of force, we could prevail and save our South Vietnamese friends from the fate of Communism. I had the training, experience and motivation, and was ready, willing and able to do my part. Screening for command meant I most surely would have the chance to join the battle.

Selling a Home in the Winter

It was the middle of winter January 1964, Virginia Beach, Virginia and houses were not moving. I had priced our house low to be sure it moved. I was going to sell it myself without a realtor as I always did. One perspective buyer came through the house and said, "What's the matter with this house?" I said, "Nothing is wrong, what do you mean?" He said, "Why is the price so low?" After he left, I raised the price and sold the house within the week. The Navy movers came and packed us out.

Jane and I loaded Paul, two years old; Becky, five; Emily, six; Cathy, eight; Krista, nine; and Debbie, eleven; our few belongings and faithful dog, Herbie, into our 1962 Chevy. We departed for our new West Coast adventure with the "Beep-Beep," our Hillman

Jane, Emily, Papa , Paul, Krista, Becky and Cathy, Lemoore

Husky, in tow. It was a fun trip, I'm sure, because I do not recall any real disasters. We headed southwest stopping at the Grand Canyon and Luke Air Force Base in New Mexico to see Captain Ron "Gunga" Dinn and family. This was to be my last visit with him. He would die within the year, after losing control of a F104, while taking off at Luke Air Force Base.

From Luke AFB we headed to Naval Air Station Lemoore, California, which would be our home base for the next two and a half years. We looked at Navy housing but instead bought a nice three bedroom home in Lemoore from Red Beck, a local builder. Jane enrolled the school-age children into the local Catholic School, Mary Immaculate Queen, and I checked into the Replacement Air Group at NAS Lemoore.

A4 Skyhawk Replacement Air Group (RAG), VA-125

February 1965. I was surprised, the replacement squadron VA-125 was short of students and they had signed me up for the full replacement course. I'd flown the Skyhawk as Operations Officer for a full two year tour in VA-81, prior to my tour at Armed Forces Staff College. I argued that Light Attack Squadron 153 was deployed in combat without an Executive Officer, my future position, and I should get out there in a hurry. USS Coral Sea with VA-153 had deployed in December 1964. The VA-153 Commanding Officer, Commander Pete Mongilardi, had been "fleeted up" to Air Wing Commander, Commander Harry Thomas, his Executive Officer, was now Commanding Officer of VA 153 leaving the squadron without an Executive Officer.

Commander Forgy, Commanding Officer, of VA-125, the training squadron, was unsympathetic and said, "Commander Leue' they don't need a squadron XO deployed, why don't you

just wait until the ship comes back in July or August?" I said, "Well, they're in combat! What happens if the Skipper is shot down?"

It didn't make sense to me, but I was stuck. I pushed as hard as I could and got through the training in a couple of months.

CDR Dave Leue, Fallon Nevada, April 1965

Fallon Nevada, Weapons Training

The next to last phase of my training was a weapons deployment to Fallon, Nevada. I was in a flight of four Commanders, consisting of Commanders Homer Smith, John Duck, John Abbott and myself. We were all heading for Light Attack squadrons as Executive Officers. Our instructor, Lieutenant Commander Ted Kaupfman gave us maximum leeway to develop and practice tactics, which we would use in Vietnam. We spent 10 days in Fallon flying three hops a day bombing, strafing and practicing tactics. I had studied the new Russian surface to air missile, the SA-2, while still in VA-81, so I shared my knowledge of the SA-2 with this group. We developed and practiced tactics designed to counter and kill the SA-2.

Carrier Qualifications

The last phase of training was carrier qualification in the A4C. My logbook shows I flew from Lemoore and completed 17 refresher day landings May 10, 1965, on board USS Kitty Hawk, CVA 63.

After day qualifying, I visited with my buddy, CDR Fred Nevett, now the Air Boss of USS Kitty Hawk. Fred and I had flown together in VF-24 in Korea.

USS Kitty Hawk CVA-63

Later, after dark I was manned up and ready to launch for my night refresher landings, when the ship experienced an arresting gear casualty. The Captain cancelled further operations and I was sent back to Lemoore, without any night landings. I checked my log book and realized I had made night landings on USS Forrestal within the year. Technically, I was still qualified. I went to see Commander Forgy. I proposed he send me directly to Westpac and the USS Coral Sea, without any night refresher landings. I showed him my logbook, which confirmed I had made night carrier landings, on USS Forrestal within the past year. Reluctantly, Commander Forgy said, "OK Leue' I'll send you, but you better not screw up."

I immediately made arrangements to fly to Manila.

CHAPTER FOUR

Off To War, USS Coral Sea

May 1965

Sunday, May 9, 1965. My bags were packed. I had my orders in hand to become Executive Officer of Navy Light Attack Squadron 153 on USS Coral Sea CVA-43. Lieutenant Gary Starbird volunteered to fly me from Naval Air Station Lemoore to NAS Alameda, California in an AD-5 Skyraider. My tickets were on a Pan Am flight, a 747, from San Francisco to Manila. I said an emotional good-by to Jane and our six children. Jane had seen me off to war many times before in Korea, this was a first for the children.

The carrier USS Coral Sea was operating in the Gulf of Tonkin off of Vietnam. It had been deployed since December 1964, actively involved in the developing Vietnam conflict. Gary Starbird dropped me off at NAS Alameda Operations. He thought nothing of giving up his Sunday just to help out a Navy buddy. Gary Starbird was the kind of guy that you wanted with you when you went to war. He would later show up on USS Coral Sea as the Air Wing 15 Landing Signals Officer.

USS Coral Sea, CVA 43

I thanked Gary and he wished me luck. I called a taxi for San Francisco International and my flight to Manila. Later, after takeoff on the long flight across the Pacific, I settled back and reflected on the growing Vietnam conflict.

I was eager to assume my new position and get into the fight. However, this would be a different fight from Korea. There, we had frontlines and regular troops in conventional combat. Vietnam was an insurgency, there were no front lines. North Vietnam was actively trying to infiltrate and overthrow the South Vietnamese government.

I had recently graduated from the Armed Forces Staff College where we had studied Vietnam in-depth. Vietnam was a political war, another of the Soviet backed, "Small Wars Of Liberation." Our true enemy was the Soviet Union. I had learned that in 1954, one million religious, Catholic, Buddhist and Confucian, had fled from North Vietnam to South Vietnam when the French departed and Ho Chi Minh took over North Vietnam. There was no religious freedom in North Vietnam.

Who would protect these people if we didn't?

The Iron Curtain covered much of Europe. "Progressives" in Europe and America generally mirrored the Soviet propaganda line. This segment of the press had already created confusion within the minds of the American people by concentrating on the problems with the Buddhist community in South Vietnam. The press never mentioned the total lack of religious freedom under the Communist in the north. In 1963, President Kennedy had ordered a CIA operation against President Ngo Diem of South Vietnam. Diem was assassinated in this operation!

This was appalling. What was Kennedy thinking? Diem had fought the French, the Japanese, the French again and now the Communist for many years. Scores of his village chiefs were being assassinated by Viet Cong sent south by Ho Chi

Minh. Had we deposed Diem because he was not nice enough about his response to this terror?

After Diem's assassination, Ho Chi Minh was reputed to say, "I can't believe the Americans could be so stupid."

A month later President Kennedy was assassinated by Lee Harvey Oswald, a Communist just returned from Russia.

It was obvious, the U.S. had a tough road ahead to maintain a free Vietnam. South Vietnam needed a strong leader to replace Diem and we needed to stop the flow of Soviet weapons of war into Haiphong and South Vietnam. Of course, a most important requirement in any conflict is total support of the American people, as we had in WWII. Without this support our cause would surely be lost.

The U. S. had the power to stop the flow of weapons from Russia and China, but not by half measures. Would the Navy be given the freedom to stop the Russian ships or mine Haiphong? Did we have the political will? Would the press focus on the Communist oppression in North Vietnam and support our efforts? Or would they just highlight the problems in the South?

These questions coursed through my mind as I flew west.

Soon enough I was in Manila. I bummed a ride on a Navy transport to NAS Cubi Point in the Philippines.

May 10, 1965. Light Attack Squadron 153. Once in NAS Cubi Operations I found a VAH-2 A3 Sky Warrior pilot filing a flight plan for USS Coral Sea. I asked him for a ride. He said, " I just have an empty jump seat in back of me. It's cramped, no place for a Commander, it won't be very comfortable." I said, " No sweat."

I got my first Coral Sea carrier landing riding backwards in an A3.

After landing I went below to VA-153's pilot's Ready Room.

The Skipper, CDR Harry Thomas, welcomed me aboard. He was of medium build, well put together, with sandy hair and a pleasant, confident smile. He was obviously pleased I was aboard. Now he had an XO, his number two, to carry the administrative burden and another senior combat leader.

I found Harry had also fought in Korea, but had night attack experience, which I did not. Later, I would learn night attack techniques from him.

CDR Harry Thomas

Observing the squadron pilots and enlisted men it was clear they respected and admired Skipper Thomas.

I had never served on this class of carrier. The ready rooms on Coral Sea were right under the flight deck athwart ship (crossway), a very convenient location. The USS Coral Sea, a Midway class ship, was the third built, following Midway and FDR. This class of ships were built very tough. All reflected the damage experience from the Kamikaze attacks on our carriers off Okinawa in WWII. They were the first US Navy carriers with armored flight decks, with extensive compartmentation and twelve fire rooms for the boilers. Midway was larger than the Essex class that I had flown from in Korea, but smaller than the Forrestal class I had flown from in the Mediterranean.

Next I met Lieutenant Commander Jim Snyder, Operations Officer. Jim was tall, thin with deep set eyes and a laconic sense of humor. Jim had been performing my duties as the Executive Officer for several months while waiting for me to arrive. He was a "no nonsense" officer who was direct and effective. I would find he was steady as a rock in combat.

Jim debriefed me on the administrative and discipline duties of the XO as he saw them. He introduced me to Lieutenant Commander

Walker Lambert who had functioned as Operations Officer while Jim was performing the duties of Executive Officer. Walker greeted me with a broad smile. He was almost as tall as Jim Snyder and he had a reserved demeanor. I would find he was a steady, confident officer, and fearless in battle.

Jim Snyder escorted me to my quarters, a single room on the second deck in the passageway populated with VA-153 officers. This was the first single room of my career, a luxury compared to the forty-two man bunkroom I experienced as an Ensign during Korea. I was exhausted. I quickly unpacked and slept the night through.

Next morning after breakfast, I found my way to the squadron ready room. Lieutenant Commander Bill Majors, the squadron Maintenance officer introduced himself. Bill was a tall, easy-going southern gentleman with an "All American" boyish grin. Others had told me Bill had been shot down earlier and rescued. In the process of his rescue it was revealed he was flying with boxer shorts emblazoned with red hearts given to him by his wife. This became a squadron joke. I would learn Bill was quiet, calm, cool and diligent in his duties as maintenance officer.

Bill introduced me to his assistants, Lieutenant Bill Smith and Lieutenant Junior Grade Walt Dill. Lieutenant Smith, the non-flying full-time Maintenance Officer was of medium build, handsome, quiet and confident. Walt Dill, his assistant, was tall, thin and unassuming. Smith and Dill were the real power behind the superb maintenance of the squadron's twelve A4C. Walt had come up through the ranks and been commissioned based on his outstanding, dedicated service.

Lieutenant Chuck McNeil, the squadron's Landing Signals Officer, tall with a broad smile, greeted me. He related his narrow escape the previous month. His A4 was hit by flak as he was attacking a bridge. His wingman called, "You have fire on the tail." He headed toward the water as his aircraft became uncontrollable. McNeil attempted to eject. His ejection seat did not fire. He then jettisoned the canopy and attempted to bail out, but was pinned against his seat by the blast of the slipstream in his spinning and burning aircraft. Miraculously, he fought free. He opened his chute just above the waves.

His troubles were not over. Landing in the water just past the surf, the Vietnamese began shooting from the beach. He swam frantically out to sea as his squadron mates strafed the gunners on the beach. Finally, an Air Force amphibian landed on the water near him and rescued him.

I was told of the squadron's first pilot killed, Lt Bill Roark. The circumstance of his loss was almost identical to Chuck McNeil's, but did not end as well. He was hit and bailed out almost directly over the beach, he landed on the beach and was shot by the North Vietnamese and was not recovered.

Later, I was introduced to Commander Air Wing 15, Commander Pete Mongilardi, the former Commanding Officer of the squadron. He had been "Fleeted Up" to Air Wing Commander on board Coral Sea in April. He was tall, thin and

wiry, obviously Italian, with dark penetrating eyes. I had previously heard of his aggressive leadership of the squadron and how he returned from the strike on Bach Long Vi Island with his aircraft so shot up it was not repairable.

CDR Pete Mongilardi, CAG-15

CDR Mongilardi related to me that he would not have made it back to the ship on that strike if it wasn't for the timely assistance of Lieutenant Howie Alexander, who directed him to

CDR Mongilardi, LTJG Greene, LTJG Keesey, LCDR McNeil, LTJG Dahl, CDR Thomas

the tanker. Despite Howie's own severe flak damage and low fuel state, he backed out of the tanker so Commander Mongilardi could refuel before flaming out. Lieutenant Alexander was awarded his first Distinguished Flying Cross for this performance. Commander Mongilardi also related how Lieutenant Alexander had single-handedly knocked down the very narrow and critical Xom Ca Trang bridge with a Bull Pup radio controlled missile. For that feat Lieutenant Alexander had been awarded his second Distinguished Flying Cross.

This was indeed a talented squadron.

Xom Ca Trang Bridge

I quickly settled into the routine of the Executive Officer of Light Attack Squadron 153 on USS Coral Sea. During my first days aboard, before I flew, I observed the squadron pilots closely as they briefed, manned

LT. Howard Alexander

aircraft, launched and recovered. They were calm, good-natured and professional as they went about their day and night combat missions. I looked forward to being the Executive Officer and Commanding Officer of this fine squadron.

Attack Squadron 153 had twelve A4C Skyhawks, 15 pilots, non-flying air intelligence and maintenance officers and approximately 150 enlisted. VA-153 was organized in the typical Navy squadron fashion. All pilots had collateral duties such as Administrative Officer, Operations Officer, Maintenance Officer, Executive Officer and Commanding Officer. The enlisted were highly trained in each of their required skills: engine mechanics, airframe mechanics, avionics technicians, ordinance men, yeomen, cooks and bakers. The Chief Petty Officers had ten to fifteen years experience in carrier squadrons. They knew aircraft maintenance, flight deck operations and the ship well. The Commanding Officer and Executive Officer usually had at least fifteen years experience in carrier squadrons. They were responsible for the leadership and welfare of the crew. I could clearly see, this crew took fierce pride in their squadron.

Air Wing Fifteen consisted of two fighter squadrons, VF-154 flying F8 Crusaders and VF-151 flying F4 Phantoms; two light attack squadrons, VA-153 flying A4C Skyhawks and VA-155 flying the newer A4E Skyhawks; one propeller attack squadron, VA-165 flying propeller driven AD-6 Skyraiders; and a Heavy attack/tanker squadron, VAH-2 flying the large twin engine A-3 Sky warrior. In addition, there were smaller detachments for early warning and jamming, from VAW-11 flying propeller driven E-2W and a reconnaissance/photo detachment from VFP-63 flying F8P Crusaders.

Rules of Engagement. In my briefings, I learned the rules of engagement (ROE) that governed our air operations, what targets we could hit or must avoid. The carrier navy's task was to operate off of North Vietnam and stop the flow of supplies. It was obvious to all, if the Navy was given the freedom to stop the Russian ships few supplies could get through. There was only one rail line to China and the war would end in short order. This freedom was never offered.

LTJG O.J. Greene

After off loading in Haiphong harbor, the supplies were transported, primarily by truck, at night, down Route 1, Routes 8 and 15 over Mugia and Bartolome passes into Laos and Cambodia. Then they could be moved with little danger from air attack to Viet Cong and North Vietnamese troops in South Vietnam. There were many other restrictions. We were not allowed to bomb the docks at Haiphong nor Russian or Soviet Block ships.

Basically, the rules of engagement only allowed us to attack the transportation structure, the roads, railroads, trains, trucks, bridges, flak sites and tunnels of North Vietnam. We weren't allowed to attack normal wartime high value targets, such as the ships bringing the weapons of war to Vietnam, the docks, power plants, military headquarters, missile sites, major ports or population.

Occasionally, major targets such as military barracks or a major bridge or air fields were assigned by the Joint Chiefs of Staff (JCS.) These were called, "Alfa Strikes." An Alfa Strikes would involve up to 30-40 aircraft of all types, all with specific missions.

The fighters had a dual mission of protecting the strike aircraft against Migs and flak suppression. Light Attack were the strike leaders and dive bombers. The Airborne Early Warning (AEW) provided missile or Mig warnings and jammed the North Vietnamese surveillance and gunfire radar.

The Air Wing was occasionally allowed to attack the North Vietnamese air fields, therefore very few Migs had been seen in the air to date and the Air Wing had lost no aircraft to Migs.

May 17, 1965. First Combat. Despite the restrictions, I went into battle with high spirits. I was now part of an outstanding Naval Attack Squadron. I was at the peak of my aviation skills, thirty seven years old, a hundred mission veteran of Korea, with over three thousand flight hours and five hundred carrier

landings. I believed passionately in our mission. I had the strong love and support of Jane and my family.

I had the normal fears of combat. This was my first combat as a senior leader. My greatest fear was that I would make a stupid mistake that jeopardized others. Also, I did fear capture.

I flew two missions on the 17th of May. These were "Armed Reconnaissance" missions. On this type mission, we flew a specific route attacking targets of opportunity and gaining intelligence. These missions

Keesey, Kraus, Bennett, McNeil, Snyder

allowed me to get the feel of the ships launch and recovery routines, learn the squadron pilots, study the terrain, experience the flak, and establish myself as a combat leader in the squadron. They were similar to the Korean combat I knew, however, tactics had changed and there was more and heavier flak, much of it radar controlled.

On one these missions, with my wingman, Lieutenant Junior Grade Steve Cole, I tried using the new "Snake Eye" retarded 500 pound bomb on a bridge. This weapon could be dropped as low as fifty feet, great for accuracy, but definitely poor for longevity. We were greeted by many orange balls of fire from several 37-mm sites protecting the bridge. The air wing had suffered heavy losses using these tactics, and had quickly reverted to steep dive bombing from medium altitude (so did I!)

Officers, Light Attack Squadron 153, embarked USS Coral Sea early 1965, CDR Mongilardi CO

Top Row. LTJG Walt Dill, LTJG Steve Cole, LTJG Paul Reyes, LCDR Bill Majors, CDR Harry Thomas, CDR Pete Mongilardi, LCDR Jim Snyder, LCDR Walker Lambert, LT Chuck McNeil, LTJG Bill Kraus, LTJG Bill Smith

Bottom Row. LTJG Lester Parmenter, LTJG Dan Dahl, LTJG Ivan Kessey, LTJG J. Peacock, LT Howie Alexander, LTJG O.J. Greene, LT Skip Bennett, LT Bill Roark

USS Coral Sea A4C waves off

Dive bombing gave enemy gunners minimum time to track and hit us. I knew from Korea to "jink," that is, fly erratically when under fire or near known gun sites.

It was true, if you went low, even low and fast, they were going to hit you. The big difference from my Korean experience was the more intense anti-aircraft fire of all sizes, 37-mm, 57-mm rapid fire (streams of orange and red balls of fire) and the crew served 85-mm. These later guns, a development of the famous German 88, were always found in a seven gun riveted circles, with a fire control in the center. All seven guns fired simultaneously, at five to seven second intervals, spitting flames thirty feet from the muzzle, exploding with an ugly black burst, up to any altitude we could fly.

The month of May went quickly. I concentrated on learning and performing my duties as Executive Officer to Commander Thomas. The flying tempo was high. We frequently flew 2, two hour missions a day. It was amazing we flew though so much flak with little damage.

O.J. Greene Flak damage

The Air Wing lost another aircraft in May, an F8 fighter from VF-154, pilot Lieutenant Kardell, KIA. It was obvious, using the current rules of engagement and tactics, we would continue to lose aircraft and pilots at a steady rate, with little return, Our targets were primarily bridges and barges. Lots of flak. In general, we were not successful in stopping the flow of supplies south. The North Vietnamese hid their trucks during the day when we were dominant, they repaired the bridges and then drove all night.

On May 21st, Rear Admiral Eddie Outlaw, our embarked Carrier Division Commander, ordered an all-out effort to stop the Vietnamese trucks going south at night. USS Coral Sea launched twenty-four A4, twelve A4C from VA-153 and twelve A4E from VA-155, on a single night launch. I was scheduled as the spare, a sure thing. Lieutenant Skip Bennett downed his aircraft, the next thing I knew I was taxiing to the catapult, BANG, I was airborne. The rendezvous with twenty four aircraft on a black night was 'hairy.' We found few trucks. However, now I was night qualified.

On 26 May I flew my last combat mission, number fourteen, without major incident or notable result. Somewhere, half way around the world, Communist munitions workers were pleased. We had improved their standard of living.

We were ordered to return to the States with a return to Vietnam in six months. Now, at least I had recent combat experience under my belt. I was prepared to lead the squadron when it returned. However, none of us knew what lay ahead.

It was best we did not know.

CHAPTER FIVE

All Hands Party

June 1, 1965. Going Home

The Coral Sea was ordered to Yokosuka, Japan, to off load aircraft and ammunition. Our aircraft and ammunition would be passed on to the next carrier scheduled for Vietnam. We were heading home!

The ship had deployed in December, 1964. I was glad I had pushed to get out here and become part of the squadron in combat, however briefly. The ship and squadron would be going back to Vietnam in six to nine months, now I had some experience in this war and I was in position to lead.

Sano Hotel Tokyo

The ship began off loading our aircraft and ammunition in Yokosuka, several days before our departure for the USA.

Pete Mongilardi, Harry Thomas and I decided to go to Tokyo for one last liberty. We took the train from Yokosuka and stayed downtown at the Hotel Sano, a four star hotel reserved exclusively for US Military forces. We had a fun evening visiting various bars, celebrating going home. Pete Mongilardi made a big pitch for a ceramic White Horse adorning one Japanese bar, but the owner would not relinquish it. (Why do I recall that?)

The next morning, Harry Thomas and I had breakfast in the Sano dining room. As we were leaving breakfast, Admiral Outlaw, Commander Carrier Group Three, who had been embarked in Coral

Sea through out the cruise, called out, "Hey, Harry!" from across the room. I kept walking because I didn't know the Admiral personally and he had called Harry by name.

When Skipper Thomas came back he looked pale. I said, "What's the matter, Skipper?"

RADM Eddie Outlaw and CDR Harry Thomas

He said, "We're going back!" I said, "I know, we're going back to the States day after tomorrow, right?"

Harry said, "No, we are going back to Vietnam day after tomorrow. President Johnson has turned Coral Sea around!!"

Instead of mining Haiphong Harbor, the President had decided to increase our forces to three aircraft carriers in the Gulf of Tonkin. He ordered Coral Sea back into battle.

As Harry Thomas and I rode the train back to the ship in Yokosuka, he was quiet and taciturn. He'd already been gone from his family for over six months. His squadron had already had twenty-five percent of his aircraft shot down, now he was going back into battle.

I blurted out, "It's our job Harry." As soon I said it, I felt bad. I'd been gone less than two months, I had no right to say a thing.

June 5, 1965. All Hands Party

There was a strict rule in the old Navy. Officers should not fraternize with enlisted men. This is a good rule. You cannot go on liberty and be friends with someone you may have to order to do dangerous or disgusting tasks the next day. An exception to this rule was the "All Hands Party." Periodically, for instance, at the end of a cruise, officers and crew would get together at an "All Hands Party" as a "thank you" for the crew's hard work and dedication. I never was fond of these parties because there was free liquor. Navy men, far from home and full of liquor, have always been a problem, myself included.

Yokosuka Allied Armed Forces Club

The VA-153 All Hands Party was held the night before we were to get underway, at the Yokosuka Allied Armed Forces Club. It was a typical all hands party with the added factor the crew knew they were not going home anytime soon.

It was a rousing party. This was a great way to say "thank you" to the crew. They had done such a great job. But, sure enough, two of our best Second-Class Aviation Machinist Mates didn't take kindly to the remarks of the Marine gate guards returning to the ship. They got in a fight defending the Navy's honor, won the fight, but ended up in the Marine Brig in Yokosuka.

This was a serious Court Martial offense.

We were going back into combat. We needed these two machinist mates in the worst way. They would work eighteen hour days keeping our aircraft flying. There was no way that the squadron could get along without these Petty Officers. I also felt we had some responsibility for getting them into this situation. Free booze was a trap.

As Executive Officer, this was now my problem. I went to the ship's Executive Officer, Commander Hoover, and explained our dilemma. I proposed that the ship get our machinist mates released from the Marine Brig and let the USS Coral Sea handle the discipline of these men with non-judicial punishment, Captain's Mast. When on board ship, a Squadron Commanding Officer always relinquished his discipline privileges to the Ship's Captain, so I needed the XO's approval. The ship's XO approved my plan.

I summoned Lieutenant Junior Grade Ivan Keesey, the VA-153 legal officer. I directed Ivan to arrange for the release of our machinist mates, the discipline would be handled within our ship. He carried out this order promptly and brought our Petty Officers back aboard.

I was very busy with other details concerning loading the ship with our replacement aircraft, ordinance and other supplies. Ivan Keesey came back to me and said, "XO, what should I do with his paperwork concerning our men that I got out of the Marine brig?" I said, "Mr. Keesey, take it to the legal office!"

I was rather irritated that he would even ask me. Well, Ivan misunderstood my instructions to take the paperwork to the <u>Ship's</u> legal office, instead, he took the paperwork to the <u>Marine's</u> legal office. A major error.

Our Petty Officers were charged with assault on the Marine gate guards, a serious court-martial offense. What we had done was to bypass the court-martial and change the punishment to non-judicial, a minor offense. I had very good reason for doing this and would do it again in a heartbeat. We needed those Petty Officers in the worst way, but the last thing I wanted was to have the

USS Coral Sea CVA-43

paperwork fall into the Marine's hands. I would find out the consequences later.

June 6, 1965. The USS Coral Sea sailed again for the Tonkin Gulf and Vietnam combat.

What lay in the future was fortunately hidden from us.

CHAPTER SIX

Commander Pete Mongilardi

June, 1 1965. The Navy, thinking the USS Coral Sea was departing for the United States, transferred our well maintained airplanes to other squadrons remaining in the Far East. Now, the Navy scurried around for replacement aircraft for us.

We received twelve ratty aircraft from other Navy and Marine A4 squadrons and aircraft pools. They were the worst A4Cs I'd ever seen. Obviously, we received everyone's problem aircraft. Now they became our problem.

Our maintenance crews set to work. My pilot's logbook shows I flew two test hops on June 10 from Naval Air Station Atsugi, Japan testing the repairs on our replacement aircraft. Other squadron pilots were busy doing the same.

June 10, 1965. The USS Coral Sea set sail for Okinawa. The ship operated for 10 days off of Okinawa trying to get our aircraft, pilots and crew back into shape. My log book shows I flew five training flights during this period.

The last night we went ashore for liberty at the White Beach, Okinawa, Officer's Club. There was a nickel slot machine in the officers club. All squadron pilots put up ten dollars of nickels. We overwhelmed the machine and won piles of nickels. This was the only machine I've ever beaten in my life. A bad omen.

The next day, the USS Coral Sea with Carrier Air Wing 15 sortied for the Golf of Tonkin and Vietnam combat.

First Mission Back

June 25, 1965. Our first missions were scheduled in the early afternoon. I was to lead a two plane armed reconnaissance flight with LTJG Dan Dahl as my wingman. Our route for this mission was the main highway, Route 1, from below the city of Vihn, north to the city of Than Hoa.

CDR Pete Mongilardi, Commander Air Wing 15, had been skipper of the VA-153 "Blue Tail Flies" for over a year. He probably had 40 to 50 combat missions. I was just getting to know him, but found he had the reputation as being aggressive and courageous in battle. He had been an outstanding squadron skipper and the squadron loved him. He continued to fly with the Blue Tails. This first day back, he was scheduled to lead a two plane armed reconnaissance flight with LTJG Paul Reyes as his wingman.

CDR Mongilardi, LTJG Dahl

All four of us sat next to each other in the front row of the ready room receiving the weather briefing and the intelligence briefing, including the location of known flak sites. I planned to fly an erratic route at varying altitudes and headings searching for targets of opportunity.

All of our aircraft were armed with two Mark 83 1000 pound low drag bombs. This was not a good load for armed reconnaissance. I would've preferred 5 inch high velocity aircraft rockets (HVAR) or six 500 pound bombs on triple bomb racks (TERS). Thousand pound bombs would be better for a bridge strike. Therefore, I picked out a bridge along the route and explained to LTJG Dahl that if we didn't find any targets of opportunity for our 1000 pound bombs on our route, we would bomb this bridge.

Commander Mongilardi overheard my comments and suggested that since I had a bridge target picked out, why not go as a four plane flight? I preferred to lead my own flight but of course agreed, after all, he was the Air Wing Commander. I felt confident, Lieutenants Junioe Grade Paul Reyes and Dan Dahl had reputations as steady and courageous wingmen.

We manned aircraft for our first mission back.

After we started engines and the ship turned into the wind, I noticed that none of my pressure instruments (airspeed, altimeter, rate of climb) were jumping as they always did when aircraft up ahead were being catapulted.

I said to myself, "My airspeed and altimeter probably aren't working." Good judgment dictated I down the airplane. But this was my first mission back and my first with the Air Wing Commander. No way was I going to down my plane. The weather was good and I knew I could fly the airplane without airspeed and altimeter.

I taxied onto the catapult. BANG, I was airborne. Sure enough, no airspeed, altimeter or pressurization. I said nothing and joined with CAG and his wingman, Lieutenant Junior Grade Paul Reyes. Lieutenant Junior Grade Dan Dahl joined on my wing. We climbed over the gulf northwest toward North Vietnam. Dan Dahl came on the air and said, "My drop tank is not transferring." I replied, "Deploy your RAT"(Ram Air Turbine).

This was the procedure to remedy a non-transferring drop tank. Dan did this, but a short time later he reported that his drop tank was still not transferring. I told him, "Return to the ship, orbit overhead until we return, jettison your ordinance in a clear area on safe."

Obviously, our crew hadn't gotten all the bugs out of our ratty replacement aircraft.

CAG Mongilardi, Paul Reyes and I proceeded as a flight of three. CAG began the reconnaissance north, starting just north of the city of Vihn on Route 1, which runs roughly north-south near the coast.

I set up a loose weave about a quarter-mile behind CAG and Paul Reyes looking for targets of opportunity. In thirty minutes we came to the end of this route without finding any targets. CDR Mongilardi said, "OK Blue Tail Three, take us to your bridge." I assumed the lead turning inland, navigating to the bridge. I found the bridge, to my surprise it had already been destroyed. I passed the lead back to CAG and slid back to number three.

The weather was a broken layer at about 3000 or 4000 feet, I couldn't tell exactly, because I had no altimeter. CAG turned north toward the city of Than Hoa.

Shortly, I spotted a hydro power plant off to my right, a perfect target for my two 1000 pounds bombs. I rolled on my back to the right and called CAG, "This is Blue Tail Three, I am rolling in on the hydro power plant off to the right." As I started my dive CAG transmitted, "Negative, negative. Power plants are not authorized targets."

I broke off my dive, pulling out to the left looking for CAG and Paul Reyes. At that time CAG transmitted, "I've got a small bridge to the left, I'm rolling in." Immediately, I heard him say, "Flak!"

Seconds later I heard a mike key and the sound of deep breathing. I assumed he had been hit. I called him, he did not answer. I called Paul Reyes and asked, "Do you have CAG?" He replied, "Negative, I lost him in the rain shower in the dive."

I called CAG repeatedly with no answer. I rendezvoused with Paul and said, "Show me the bridge CAG dove on." The rain shower had moved and Paul led me to the bridge.

Paul and I dove on the same bridge to the south as CAG had. I pulled out low hoping to see smoke, CAG's aircraft wreckage or parachute, so we could set up a rescue.

Paul and I repeatedly jinked our way through rain showers and flak from the same site that had hit CAG. We dove in different directions and from different altitudes, but we never saw a thing, no smoke, no parachute, no wreckage.

Nothing.

I'm not sure how long Paul Reyes and I searched, but suddenly I came to my senses.

My fuel was down close to below 3000 pounds! We had a rule, always depart for the ship no lower than 4000 pounds. We called this, "Bingo." It gave us 1500 to 2000 pounds at the ship, enough for a couple of passes at the deck.

I called for the A3 tanker, which fortunately was just off the coast about twenty miles away. I had some trouble finding the tanker, I was without an altimeter or airspeed.

I finally found the tanker and joined up. The A3 tanker streamed his basket. The tanker pilot asked me to relay the situation on CAG so he could pass the information to the ship on his high frequency transmitter.

When my refueling probe hit the tankers basket, the basket reeled in. This happened infrequently. The solution was, the tanker had to speed up. I called the tanker pilot repeatedly, "Speed Up! your basket is retracting." The tanker pilot was apparently busy talking on his high-frequency radio relaying information to the ship. We were at dangerously low fuel states. I waited, the tanker did not speed up.

I called Paul Reyes, his fuel state was a little better than mine. I said, "Tank if you can, I have got to depart for the ship!"

Finally, I blew off my external tank and climbed for the ship praying that I could make it. I went as high as the A4 would go, maybe forty thousand? Without pressurization my canopy iced over and I had to scratch the ice off with my protractor to see out. I rolled on my back repeatedly and finally I saw the ship, dropped my speed brakes, dove for the ship, lined up in the ship's wake with my fuel state near zero. I dropped my gear, flaps and fortunately had an angle of attack indicator for my approach speed. I had a head cold to boot, my ears were bursting as I rocketed toward the ship on final.

Through my plugged up ears I heard the Landing Signals Officer (LSO) yelling, "Put your hook down!!"

I put my arresting hook down and slammed aboard. I didn't have enough fuel for a wave off. This was the first and only "no-hook pass" (Forgetting to put my hook down) of my career. I owed Chuck McNeil a bottle. (Tradition for no hook passes). Paul Reyes was able to tank and came aboard shortly thereafter.

I debriefed and wrote up my reports. Harry Thomas said he couldn't believe that Pete Mongilardi was gone. He said, "I'm sure he'll come back."

Personally, I knew he was dead, I heard CAG get hit and I figured he went straight in. Killed on a lousy worthless bridge. (This turned out be the case, later North Vietnamese papers published pictures of the crash with graphic descriptions of the pilots injuries.)

I didn't relate this information to Harry at that time. I knew he felt bad enough, he had been Pete Mongilardi's XO for over a year, most of it in combat. They were very close.

We were back in combat. This definitely was not a good start.

CHAPTER SEVEN

Night Attacks, Alpha Strikes

Commander Wesley McDonald

CDR Wesley McDonald

The day following the loss of Commander Mongilardi, I flew two day and one night mission. For the next month we would average one mission a day.

The weather was good and Coral Sea was launching maximum missions. We operated briefly without an Air Wing Commander, then Commander Wesley McDonald came aboard to take over as Commander Air Wing 15. He would prove to be a strong and personable Air Wing Commander

Notes in my logbook show that although we were flying a maximum number of missions, most of the targets concerned the transportation system, bridges, fuel storage, and occasionally ammunition storage. Mostly these were high risk, low value targets. We had some success at night when the trucks were moving. We continued to be denied the real targets, the Russian ships and the docks at Haiphong.

Night Attacks

The North Vietnamese moved almost no supplies during the day because of our dominance in the air. But, they moved plenty at night. Navy carrier air wings of that era were not well equipped or well trained for night attack missions. We had no all weather attack aircraft in 1965. The Coral Sea had two A4 jet attack squadrons and one A1 propeller attack squadron. The A1 was not fast enough to survive the heavy antiaircraft fire found in North Vietnam. They were relegated to missions in South Vietnam.

The A4 squadrons, being the Navy's only resource for the work, were routinely scheduled and used for night attack. Most A4 squadrons did not like night attack missions, they patrolled at above 5000 feet, where you can't see blacked out trucks. They were not effective. Night carrier operations in a single piloted jet fighter were intimidating enough without adding the terror of streams of tracers that looked as if they would hit you between the eyes. Harry Thomas alone had some success at night. He had

done some night attack work in Korea and he pioneered the effective use of the A4 at night in Vietnam. I eagerly sought his wisdom.

We were well trained in launch and recovery at night from the carrier; the problem was finding blacked out trucks in the dark. Harry found and destroyed trucks. I quizzed him on his tactics.

CDR Harry Thomas

Harry told me, "The key to finding and killing trucks is counter-intuitive." He said, "To find trucks at night you have to first locate a destroyed bridge or a ferry crossing on a main route or connecting route during the day time. Mark that point on your chart. Now at night, find a good coast in point that you can identify on radar, like Hon Me Island. Then Dead Recon (DR) navigate (time, distance & heading) from that point to your choke point, your downed bridge. Drop flares, you will usually find trucks there, but you have to go low to see them. You cannot see blacked out trucks from dive bombing altitudes of 5000 to 10,000-feet."

Harry taught me it was safer at low altitudes at night, than in the day. You had to be careful, know where you were, stay away from the known high flak concentrations, use your radar, and know the height of the terrain.

The A4C Skyhawk had a basic radar which, with proper training, gave a lot of information. The radar, designated APG-53, had a terrain clearance mode that I utilized on all night missions to gauge my height above the black hills below. Lieutenant Marv Natcheck in VA-125 had taught me how to use the radar effectively. Thanks to Marv, I knew how high I was on black nights in Vietnam. I insisted that our VA-153 radar technicians maintain our radars to the highest level and they did. If I wasn't sure of the terrain, I got out of there. A hill can kill you just as dead as an enemy bullet.

The A4C radar gave a good picture of land/water contrast, but except for terrain clearance, was not useful for navigation over land.

I expanded on Harry's tactics. After tanking I put my wingman 1000 feet above me so he became accustomed to the night and instruments. I would find a coast-in point on radar then navigate by dead reckoning, that is, by time, distance and heading, to find the area I wanted to attack.

When at the choke point, I dropped two, 2 million candlepower Mark 24 parachute flares, circled below the flares, then came down the road at 200-300 feet, at 400 to 450 knots, staying off to the right side of the road, where I could easily see the trucks through my left windscreen. I would describe the location of any trucks to my wingman. Such as, "We have ten trucks north of the bridge." Now he knew where to look when he was in his run. I then pulled up to 40 degrees on my gyro into the blackness and cleared him into his run.

My wingman would initiate a shallow dive, leveling off below 500 feet, rocket down the road, the trucks would came into view, he'd strafe with 20 mm cannon or drop 250 or 500 pounds retarded snake-eye bombs or CBU2 bomb-lets. After he had completed his run he would pitch up to 40° on his gyro into the blackness, call "Blue Tail Two, Off", and go into a left orbit at 5000 feet. I would then call "Blue Tail One, In" and repeat the attack.

This routine was repeated, dropping flares as necessary. We never saw each other except when one was under the flare, keeping track of each other by calling, "In" and "Off" the target.

To the gunners on the ground we would burst into the light at 400 plus knots, this gave them very little tracking time. At times the red balls of fire scared us, but we were poor targets. It was an acceptable risk. If the flak was heavy, we went elsewhere.

We found and burned a lot of trucks this way. Every truck full of

A. J. Foyt

ammunition and weapons we destroyed, saved some of our Army or Marine buddies fighting in the jungles to the south. When the North Vietnamese caught on to this tactic, driving their trucks rapidly from under the flare light, (We called them A. J. Foyt-ski, in honor of the great race driver), I would drop a bomb with the first flares. This got the drivers out of their trucks.

I taught this tactic to anyone who was interested. In 1965, our sister squadron on Coral Sea and many others were not. Our squadron's first tour wingmen showed great courage and faith in their leader, to operate down low at night.

We had a series of successes on night missions using this tactic. I recall one night early in 1965 with Lieutenant Junior Grade Paul Reyes on a mission at the Ron Ferry on Route One. It was a very black night with no moon or stars visible. Late in the mission, we found a string of ten to twelve trucks on the north side of the ferry crossing.

I had already expended my ordnance on other targets. Paul's aircraft was loaded with napalm. This was an ordnance load we never used at night. I believe the napalm was left on his aircraft from a day close air support mission that had been cancelled. I watched as Paul made a beautiful, on the deck, napalm drop, engulfing and destroying the trucks. Paul was an amazing, calm, courageous warrior, night and day.

July 16, 1965. Lieutenant Skip Bennett and Lieutenant Howie Alexander found and were attacking trucks on Route 1 north of Vihn. Later in the mission, Lieutenant Bennett reported, "My aircraft's been hit, I'm on-fire, I'm turning east, out to sea! "

There was a low overcast. Lieutenant Alexander told me he could see the glow from Lieutenant Bennett's burning aircraft in the overcast, as he followed him out to sea.

Bennett came back on the air saying, "Howie, I'm losing control, I'm ejecting."

Alexander dropped down below the overcast and circled the location of the ejection. Before long, he saw flares fired by Bennett in his life raft in the dark sea below.

Alexander contacted the Search and Rescue (SAR) destroyer and directed it to Bennett's location. The destroyer homed in on the flares and tracer rounds from Bennett's 38 caliber pistol in the pitch -black night.

In his excitement, Alexander pushed his transmitter switch so hard talking to the destroyer, he broke the switch and could not communicate after that with anyone. Nevertheless, he did an excellent job alerting the Search and Rescue (SAR) destroyer, and directing it to Bennett's location. LT Bennett was rescued and returned to the ship by helo the next day.

This mission had profound effect on Lieutenant Bennett. I observed him closely. Thereafter, he was still competent and effective, but no longer a "tiger" at night.

Lessons Learned

The tempo of night operations was such that I noticed a significant change in my own attitude toward night operations and carrier landings. I looked forward to them. It was a lesson in life. Only a year or so before, in the Mediterranean, on USS Forrestal, night carrier landings were terrifying to me. Now, after being shot at repeatedly over the beach, I looked forward to the night carrier landing as the fun part.

I got better in battle. I recall overstaying my time attacking trucks, returning at full power to make my expected approach time (EAT). We were marshalling overhead just off of Hainan Island. I started my decent just barely on time when I realized I was penetrating 180 degrees from the proper bearing. I rolled into a split "S," coming out on the proper bearing without losing my place.

July 17, 1965. Alpha Strikes

Than Hoa Bridge, Vietnam

Interspersed with our day and night reconnaissance, we flew "Alpha" strikes authorized by the JCS. One was on the infamous Than Hoa Bridge. This bridge, built by the French, was a massive steel girder bridge just north of Than Hoa on Route One, the major route along the coast running south from Hanoi.

The bridge had been attacked many times, hit and damaged, but never destroyed. It was very heavily defended by multiple flak sites. Our new Air Wing Commander, Commander Wes McDonald led this strike. Commander Harry Thomas, LCDR Jim Snyder, and myself, all led four plane divisions. Both fighter squadrons were assigned to hit the heavy anti-aircraft flack batteries surrounding the bridge and provide target combat air patrol (TARCAP).

The dives were planned from West to East down the length of the bridge at a slight angle to maximize the probability of a hit. We dove from 12,000 feet carrying two 1000 pound bombs apiece. The dive was without speed brakes at 60°. The order of attack was VA -155 first, then Commander Thomas's division, Jim Snyder's division, then mine. In my dive I could see the bridge was already covered with bomb bursts. I released my bombs aiming for the center of the smoke. I commenced my pull-out putting on seven "Gs."

Than Hoa Bridge under attack

As I bottomed out there was a tremendous explosion on my right-wing. The aircraft rolled up on its left side.

I leveled my wings. Looking right I saw a gaping hole in my wing. The A4 wing is a "wet' wing full of fuel. Thankfully it did not explode.

My wingman joined and confirmed I was rapidly losing fuel from my damaged right wing. I called for a tanker and proceeded out to sea.

I found the tanker and plugged in.

Flak Damage, Plane Captain Loftis, CDR Dave Leue July 17, 1965

We were 150 miles from the ship so I stayed plugged-in and the tanker headed for the ship with fuel pouring from my right-wing. The tanker did a great job, dropping me off at three miles aft the ship.

I dropped my gear and flaps and trapped aboard. It is a tribute to the design and construction of the great A4 Skyhawk that my airplane held together under the high stress of the pullout despite significant damage. (The Than Hoa bridge was not destroyed until hit by a Air Force 2000 pound "Smart Bomb" years later. Over 90 aircraft were shot down attacking this bridge)

August 1965.

My log book shows I flew almost 30 missions during July, a quarter of them at night. There seemed to be no let up in our tempo of operations. No one knew how long this extension of our combat would be. The restrictive rules of engagement were unchanged.

I was feeling more confident in my skills, both night and day. USS Coral Sea was one of the first carriers to get an angled deck. However, it only had three, rather than the standard, four steam catapults. The catapults were the early short catapults. These catapults were limited in their launching capability. Sometimes in the Gulf of Tonkin, when it was hot and humid with no wind, the catapult officer could not give the required 15 knots of excess end speed. He would come on the air as you wound up on the cat ready to go and say, "Blue Tail 302, I can only give you 8 knots excess, will you take it?" We always said, "OK." Usually in this circumstance, after the catapult stroke, the stick would be in my lap, there would be a little buffeting and settling, then the old A4C would accelerate and slowly climb.

August 12, 1965.

Full Moon Madness. My wingman was Lieutenant George Wilkins, an outstanding Naval Academy graduate on his first combat cruise. Our aircraft configuration was our standard: a single 400 gallon drop tank on the centerline station, right and left wing stations had a multiple bomb rack (MBR), each MBR carried three flares and three 250 pound Snake Eye retarded bombs. These were arranged with flares first on one side and bombs first on the other. We could select either bombs or flares at will.

After briefing, we manned up and launched. I had briefed our A3 tanker, which had launched ahead of us, to head out on a 310 degree bearing for the beach at 5000 feet with his green flashing recognition light on. We rendezvoused with the tanker, topped off on fuel, then I dropped down to 4000 feet, Lieutenant Wilkins was briefed to stay at 5000 feet, 1000 feet above me, as we continued to the beach. I cruised at 275 knots, lights out and called all my turns so that Lieutenant Wilkins could match them.

Hon Me Island, just off the coast near Vihn glowed on my radar. We coasted in, found Route One, then turned south.

At that time, my night vision was excellent. The moon was so bright I could see the road clearly and could read my chart.

Dropping down to 500 feet I started weaving back and forth over the road. Shortly, a long military convoy of trucks headed south came into view

This convoy had multiple trucks with long dark, low-boy trailers carrying cylindrical objects, covered in tarps.

I turned on my gun sight to its lowest setting and armed my guns.

We had fooled the North Vietnamese. Camouflaged and lights out, their trucks were used to sneaking by our attack aircraft flying at higher altitude.

"Blue Tail Two I have a convoy of trucks, I'm attacking without flares, orbit," I exclaimed to George Wilkins who was at 5000 feet above me. He acknowledged.

Making an easy right turn to the west then reversing 270 degrees to the left, I set up to attack the convoy head-on, diving to the north. My heart raced.

Commencing a shallow dive, I put my sight on the lead truck waiting until I was within 500 feet. I touched the trigger.

The satisfying din of my twin MK 12 cannons filled my ears. Tracers raced

George Wilkins -Dave Leue'

through the black night. The first two trucks exploded into flames. "Great!," I said to myself.

I pulled out just over the burning trucks then pitch up to 40 degrees on my gyro and called, "Blue Tail One is Off. Blue Tail Two hit the last trucks." George replied, "I have the fires. I'm in, diving North"

From above I could see George make a beautiful hit on the trailing trucks with his Snake-Eye 250 pound retarded bombs. Trucks and trailers exploded, burning. I said, "Great hits Two!"

Now we had them. Both ends of the convoy were enveloped in raging fires. George and I took turns methodically strafing and bombing the center of the convoy.

Burning fuel ran down the hill like molten lava. Fires shot up so high that a destroyer, 25 miles at sea, reported they could see flames. We took some scattered AAA tracer fire, but suppressed it with our 20MM.

I'm not certain what this convoy was, but I suspect that it was a Russian SA-2 surface to air missile system with its missile fuel, radar, trucks, launchers and missiles.

We continued this mayhem until we ran out of ammunition. I reported "Ammo minus," as I climbed toward the ship.

"Jehovah" (RADM Reedy, CTF-77), apparently listening, came on the air directing our A1 Skyraiders operating in South Vietnam to fly north and continue to hit this convoy. We returned to the ship and recovered individually.

It was very early in the morning when we recovered. No one, except the duty officer, was in the ready room to share our victory.

I hit the sack exhausted.

CHAPTER EIGHT

Commander Harry Thomas

Friday, August 13, 1965 .

LCDR George Wilkins and I didn't get a chance to celebrate our big truck kill from the night before. There was a crisis in the Seventh Fleet. Last night, an A4C Skyhawk from USS Midway was shot down by a Russian SA-2 missile, just north of where George Wilkins and I were burning those trucks.

For months we had watched the North Vietnamese construct Russian SA-2 missile sites near Hanoi. We were forbidden to attack them. We knew from intelligence that they also had SA-2 batteries that were camouflaged and mobile. Now, Commander Task Force Seventy Seven was finally going to act!

Harry Thomas and I had been watching the SA-2 situation develop. We discussed ways that we would attack SA-2 missile sites if we were given permission.

Our squadron had a radar homing device in four of our A4C in place of the radar. It was called the APR-23 "Red Head." The APR-23 had a screen like a radar that could be used to home on either S, C, or X-band radars. It also had an audio output, which we could use to identify the type radar.

CDR Harry Thomas

We had training tapes with sounds of various different radars. The Russian SA-2 guidance radar, "Fan Song," an

S band radar, sounded like a rattlesnake. I won't ever forget the sound.

The problem was, no one in our squadron, our technicians or pilots, had been trained on the APR-23. Fortunately, I had some training from my last squadron, Attack Squadron 81. Commander Julian Lake, Commander Air Wing Eight, had conducted the fleet evaluation of the APR-23. while I was on USS Forrestal in 1963-64. At that time, I practiced returning to the Forrestal homing on the ships radar using the APR 23.

I asked the Skipper if I could have our squadron technicians learn the APR-23 and get our APR 23 in working order, then train our pilots in its use. This would allow us to find and attack the SA- 2 missile sites when we were authorized. He approved this.

Apparently, Commander Task Force 77 (CTF-77) staff, directing USS Coral Sea and the other carriers in Vietnam, was unaware of the APR-23. The CTF-77 operations plan for Friday, August 13, 1965 called for massive low level reconnaissance missions, from USS Coral Sea and USS Midawy, looking for SA-2 missile sites visually.

Harry Thomas and I both knew this tactic was a serious mistake. It would expose many aircraft to heavy enemy AAA fire at low altitudes. Harry complained to the staff, but got no satisfaction.

An order was an order. We planned our missions to comply with the staff's guidance. All twenty-four of VA-153 and VA-155's squadron's aircraft would be used on this mission.

Commander Harry Thomas, was scheduled to lead the first flight of four from VA-153, I was schedule to lead the second flight of four and the Operations officer, Lieutenant Commander Jim Snyder, the third. We were each given a designated area to cover and told to conduct our searches at minimum altitude to avoid the SA-2 missile.

I briefed my flight that we would fly south at high altitude to the Laotian border then reverse course dropping down to the deck spreading out a-beam then make our minimum altitude search coming out of Laos, an unexpected direction. Skipper Thomas's division launched.

We manned up and started. I was taxing up the deck, passing the island toward the catapults. A sailor raced out of the island, jumped up toward my cockpit with a note. I grabbed for the note, but it was blown down the deck by a blast from a launching jet. This was highly unusual procedure. I had a bad feeling that something had happened to the Skipper.

After launching, my flight of four rendezvoused. We climbed south to 20,000 feet, then turned toward Laos. At the Laotian border, I reversed course while descending to 200 feet, heading northeast to cover our area. I spread the flight out abeam, about a quarter mile between each of my four aircraft.

We held 420 knots, hugging the earth and rolling on our backs as we went over peaks pulling down into valleys. We were within range of even the smallest weapons and were shot at the whole way. All aircraft constantly jinked right, left, up and down spoiling the gunner's aim the best we could. We swept our area from the Laotian border to the sea, searching for any evidence of SA-2 missiles. We saw no missile batteries.

Vietnam

We saw many machine guns and flak sites. Two of our aircraft were hit by machine gun fire, but with no major damage. We proceeded out to sea, found the USS Coral Sea and landed back aboard when it turned into the wind for recovery.

I was sent below to the hangar deck, where the crew used CO2 to put out a small fire in my engine compartment caused by a machine gun hit. The crew put the boarding ladder up alongside the cockpit. I was about to un-strap and get out when Wes McDonald, our Air Wing Commander came up the ladder and said, "Harry Thomas has been shot down and killed. Dave, you are the Commanding Officer of VA-153."

I always wanted to be a squadron skipper, but not this way.

I gathered my thoughts saying a quick prayer as I made my way from the hangar deck to the ready room. I had witnessed this scene twice before in Fighter Squadron 24 in Korea, when the XO took over after my Commanding Officer's were killed. I knew I had to be strong.

I met Lieutenant Bill Kraus on the way to the ready room. He had been Skipper Thomas's wingman. He told me that their flight had run into a very heavy barrage of 37-mm flak passing through an area of karst called Quang Sui. They hit the skipper's aircraft, it rolled over and crashed. There was no chance of survival.

I called all pilots to the ready room for an all pilots meeting (APM). I invited the Chief Petty Officers and senior enlisted. They were an essential part of the team, without their support I was nothing.

I said simply, "We have lost Commander Harry Thomas. He was a great leader. This is an essential squadron. We have an important mission. You've been doing a great job, its very important to the country that we carry on as before. I expect your full support. Lieutenant Commander Jim Snyder will be our XO until further notice. Any questions?"

We paused briefly for the memorial service on the hangar deck, then we resumed our combat missions.

CHAPTER NINE

Acting Commanding Officer

What now?

I reflected. To this point, the squadron had five aircraft shot down, three pilots killed, including two commanding officers. Not one of the targets we had attacked or destroyed were significant. It seemed we were in a high risk and low return war. Would this change?

VA-153 Blue Tail lads aboard USS Coral Sea   OJ Greene Photo

I was Acting Commanding Officer, nevertheless, I had all the authority and responsibility of the Commanding Officer, the Skipper.

My tactical philosophy had been closely aligned with that of Pete Mongilardi and Harry Thomas. I had always looked forward to being in Command. Was I ready? Was I up to the task? It looked easy from below. The view now was totally different. I prayed I would not make any tragic blunders.

The squadron was strong. I knew it was important that I show strength, confidence and not falter. I wrote Jane giving her all the details of Harry's death I was allowed. I informed her it was now up to her to carry the load as the Skipper's wife, keeping all squadron wives informed. I knew she would have been given the bare details of Harry's death by message and then helped Harry's wife, Marie, in her time of grief. I wrote Marie Thomas. That task was very difficult for me.

War does not stop for private tragedies. I continued to lead missions, night and day. I went to Mass daily. I prayed a lot. I had no idea how long I would be Skipper, whether I would remain "Acting CO" or be made permanent Commanding Officer. I asked CAG, he did not know. I vowed to do my best each day and not think too far ahead.

I developed a mental game long ago. I tried to concentrate only on the current "line period," or time at sea. I concentrated on making it through to the next in-port period. Mentally this was a short term goal that seem achievable. We were due into Cubi Point, the Philippines Islands in a few weeks. I concentrated on getting there with the squadron in one piece.

O. J. Greene makes LT

Morale remained high, the crew worked unceasingly to service, repair, load bombs, patch up flak holes and keep us going. Flight operations went on for 12 hours every day either noon to midnight or midnight to noon.

The crew, therefore, worked fourteen to eighteen hours a day, without complaint on the flight deck and below. If one specialty was overloaded, others stepped forward to help out. For example, at 2 AM one morning as I was passing through the hangar bay, I saw our engine mechanics swinging a replacement engine into one of our A4C in preparation for a big strike scheduled for the next day. Up on the aircraft, helping our mechanics struggle with the engine, was our squadron cook, working proudly with his big white baker's hat on, giving the engine mechanics a hand. What a team!

Anti-Sam Tactics

After losing five aircraft, and Commander Harry Thomas, on the senseless mass search for Russian surface-to-air missiles at low altitude, I was mad as hell. I went to the Admiral's Staff and requested to brief them about the squadron's capability to find and attack SAMs without massive low level raids. This was granted.

I worked out a tactic utilizing the APR-23 radar homer in conjunction with the AD5-Q electronic countermeasure aircraft we had on the Coral Sea and an A3Q electronic countermeasure based ashore.

Paul Reyes makes Lieutenant

I proposed that we operate both electronic countermeasure aircraft off the coast where we suspected a missile site was operating, then vector our APR-23 equipped A4C armed with bombs to attack the SAM site when it was detected by the electronic countermeasure aircraft. This would greatly limit the number of exposed aircraft.

This tactic was approved. I asked for a volunteer as a wingman for the first mission. Bill Kraus volunteered to go with me. The A-3Q countermeasure aircraft crew was based ashore. They flew aboard by COD (Carrier On-board Delivery) for the briefing. We reviewed our tactics. The two electronic surveillance aircraft would fly racetrack patterns roughly perpendicular to each other so when a SAM-2's radar came on the air, they could cross bearings to plot where the SAM site was located.

On our first anti-SAM mission, Bill Krause and I launched, rendezvoused and proceeded toward the Vietnam coast where we suspected a SAM site was located. The AD5-Q had been launched 15 minutes ahead of us because of its slower speed. As we approached the coast of Vietnam, we made radio contact with the A-

VA-153 A4C over the Gulf of Tonkin

3Q and the AD-5Q countermeasure aircraft.

Within a short period of time, the AD5-Q gave us a vector. We dropped down on the deck and accelerated to 450 knots. I had a strobe, like a lightning bolt on my scope. I could hear the typical rattlesnake sound of the SA-2's Fan Song radar. The strobe on my scope indicated the missile site was off to my left. We banked steeply in that direction. The strobe stayed on the left of my scope. I ended up chasing my tail with Bill Krause chasing me going 450 knots. We were banking and pulling "Gs" right on the deck. It seemed that every Vietnamese with a machine gun or a gun, was shooting at us.

My radar homing gear obviously was not working properly. From the sound of my homer and the vectors I was getting from the countermeasure aircraft, I felt we were close to the site. We spent 10 or 15 minutes, far too long, zipping around at low altitude getting shot at. I saw machine gunners in their pits frantically trying to get the correct lead on us as we rocketed by.

My aircraft was hit several times by small caliber machine guns. One armor piercing 30 caliber ricocheted off my boot heel. We never found the SAM site but, we learned a lot.

I picked up the bent bullet in the cockpit when I got back.

Commander Wes McDonald, our Air Wing Commander, arranged for a helo to take us oue sister carrier where I briefed their A4 squadrons. For the remainder of the year 1965, this tactic became the standard anti-SAM tactic. A series of SAM sites were found and destroyed using it.

On June 15, 1966 Lieutenant Commander Ted Kaupfman, VA-55, flying an A4E from USS Ranger was shot down while using this tactic leading an Air Force strike on a SA-2 site. (Ted spent seven years of torture in the Hanoi Hilton). Later, in October, Lieutenant. Paul Moore of VA-155, our sister squadron, was using this tactic when he was hit by small arms in his fuel control and in his wing tanks. His engine stuck at about 80% power and he was losing fuel rapidly. Since he had no control of his engine speed, they tried to back the A3 tanker into his refueling probe. In doing so he bent his probe up about 45°. This created a lot of drag and he slowly began to lose altitude. Finally, he had to eject.

He told me he nearly drowned when the parachute canopy covered him and started to drag him under the water. He barely freed himself using his shroud cutter knife.

This tactic was obviously imposed a high risk. It exposed the attacking aircraft to intense anti-aircraft fire from massed weapons which were always placed near SAM sites. It was all we had in 1965. The Navy would soon install electronic countermeasures in our aircraft and develop a very effective anti-SAM missile, the Shrike, designed to home on and destroy the SA-2 Fan Song radar.

The Letter from the Marines

I returned from the mission looking for SAMs, hot sweaty and frustrated. When I entered the ready room the duty officer said, "Skipper, the Ship's XO said he wanted to see you ASAP. He sounded bent out of shape." I left my flight gear on and hurried to the XO's cabin. As I entered his cabin he literally threw a letter at me. I pick it up and read it. It was from the Commander of the Marine detachment in Yokosuka. My name was prominent and it contained words such as, "worst miscarriage of Naval Justice ever witnessed..." The XO said, "Well, what are you going to do about it?" I thought a moment then said, "XO my job is to try to keep my guys alive, I'm not going to do a thing." I turned and walked out. That letter is still buried somewhere in my record.

The Ship in Vihn Harbor, Lieutenant Bill Kraus

Late in August, Commander McDonald briefed a major air wing strike deep into North Vietnam. The weather was marginal. After launch and rendezvous, we proceeded toward the target. I was leading eight A4Cs from VA 153. The deeper we penetrated into Vietnam, the worse the weather became. Finally, Commander McDonald canceled the strike and directed individual divisions to break off and attack targets of opportunity.

I broke off with four aircraft and directed the other division to find their own targets. I proceeded to the south of Vihn where I knew there was a large bridge on Route One. We dive bombed the bridge with our 1000 pound bombs. As we were pulling off of this target I saw flak erupt to the north of us near Vihn. At the same time I heard an excited exchange on the radio that sounded like Commander McDonald's voice. I called and asked, "Do you need help?" He said, "Yes!"

I proceeded north with my division and joined the fray. We made two dives strafing just to draw fire to help get CAG out of Vihn.

It was against Air Wing doctrine to attack a heavily defended target like Vihn without proper pre-planning and flak suppressors. There were hundreds of guns there. A flight of four or eight was no match for all those guns. After landing and debriefing my flight I went to Commander McDonald and expressed my concern.

CAG said, "On the way back from the target I saw a large unusual ship in Ben Thuy harbor. I felt that it may be carrying surface-to-air missiles, that's why I attacked it." We were forbidden to attack Russian or Soviet Bloc ships at sea or in Haiphong Harbor. Somehow, this ship was an exception. I didn't ask why.

"Can't we make a major strike on the ship, using flak suppressors, radar jammers, the whole package?" I asked. CAG replied, "If I ask JCS for an Alpha strike it will take a month and by that time the ship will be long gone."

I couldn't stop thinking about that ship in Vihn Harbor, it was the first ship we had been allowed to hit in the war. There had to be a way to sink that ship. I was frustrated that we wouldn't immediately mount a major strike on it.

After I thought about it for awhile, I came to the conclusion that two planes carrying Bullpup missiles could hit the ship.

The Bullpup was a 500 pound rocket propelled missile with a 250 pound warhead. It was a radio controlled missile with a range of about 2 to 3 miles. We had many very accomplished Bullpup missile shooters in VA-153. I personally had been a great advocate of this missile and had fired many in training when I was in Attack Squadron 81 on USS Forestall in the Mediterranean.

I asked for a volunteer for this mission and Lieutenant. Bill Kraus stepped forward, as he always did, for any high risk mission. I briefed CAG about my plan and he approved it.

The next day Bill Kraus and I launched late in the morning carrying two Bullpups apiece. We had practiced our skills the night before on the Bullpup missile training device in the ready room. This device was a very early video game.

My plan for the mission was to climb to 20,000 feet and proceed over the water down the coast, as if we were going to fly past Ben Thuy to a target further north. After passing Ben Thuy, Bill Kraus would break off diving first to the north, then reverse to the south launching his missile at the ship. When Bill broke off I would turn out to sea to the east then immediately reverse course diving to the West to launch my missile. Thus both missiles would be in the air at the same time coming from different directions.

It was beautiful and clear on the day of the mission. After we were airborne, Bill Kraus joined up and we proceeded down the coast past Ben Thuy, as planned. Bill Kraus broke off diving to the north then reversing left to the south, I did my 270° turn to the right and we started our dives together. The tactic worked beautifully, no flak. We surprised them.

However, when I tried to launch my missile, nothing happened. I aborted my dive, climbed back up and went through my check off list. I checked all my switches, then shook the gear handle to be sure the armament safety switch had been disengaged. I heard my 20 mm cannons go, "Thunk." This indicated that my problem was solved.

The gunners were now all alerted. As I was climbing back to the east I knew I should not make another run. I preached this time and again, "Only make one run."

Bill Kraus had made his run unscathed and had hit the ship, however the ship still appeared mostly intact.

As foolish as it was, I rolled in again. I launched my missile and was immediately greeted by a barrage of bursting black 85-mm flak. As I got closer, crisscrossing streams of red and orange balls of fire from the 57-mm and then 37-mm rapid fire guns greeted me. I held on trying to concentrate keeping the Bullpup missile's flare on the target. The volume of fire increased to a horrendous level. They were locked on to me with radar.

I realized, if I didn't jink immediately, I'd be toast. I pitched up violently then rolled on my back, jinking right and left. This threw the flak off momentarily, but I lost control of the missile and it splashed harmlessly in the water 100 feet from the ship.

Now I was mad. Everything I knew and preached about staying alive in combat, went out the window.

I climbed up and rolled in again and launched my other missile. Out of the corner of my eye, I could see that Bill Kraus had followed my poor leadership. He had commenced his second run and was surrounded by a tremendous volume of bursting flak and tracers.

The flak was worse than the last run. The flak intensity reminded

Billy Byers makes Lieutenant

me of the pictures of Kamikazes attacking the US fleet off of Okinawa in World War II. Only this time Bill Kraus and I were the Kamikazes!

I pressed on trying to concentrate, holding the Bullpup flare on the target as masses of red and orange balls of fire rose to meet me. Finally, black bursting 85 MM just overwhelmed me. I said to myself, "Leue you've got a microsecond to live, if you don't jink." I pitched up, maneuvering violently. At one time I rolled onto my back still trying to control the missile with left, right, up and down commands.

I missed the ship. Now I was in close. Flak was all around me. I turned steeply to the left pulling hard, a wall of flak following me until I was out of range.

Bill Kraus joined up on me and we flew back to the ship in silence.

On debriefing, Bill Kraus appeared visibly shaken. He related how the red and orange streams of 37 and 57 mm tracers were going by so close on either side of his cockpit he was afraid to maneuver. He said he had no idea how he could have possibly survived that mission.

I wrote him up for a Distinguished Flying Cross which, in retrospect, was at least two award levels below what I should have given him considering what he did and went through.

The ship became an obsession with me and I continued to plan how I was going to sink it.

Hitting the ship in the daytime without a major strike or without massive flak suppression seemed out of the question. I thought about hitting the ship at night, at low altitude.

We had been very successful destroying trucks at night using 250 pound or 500 pound snake eye retarded bombs. I reasoned, if we could destroy trucks at night, why not the ship? What we needed was some deception to draw the flak away from us at low altitude.

I talked to the skipper of the A3 Sky Warrior squadron and together we settled on the following tactic. Four A4C and four A3 would launch together. The A4's would rendezvous on the A3's, then in-flight refuel from them. The A3's. would then climb to 25,000 feet and proceed over Ben Thuy Harbor.

Meanwhile the A4's carrying six 500 pound snake eye retarded bombs each, would break up into two sections of two aircraft descending to 1500 feet orbit just off the coast until the A3's each dropped 10 Mark 24 flares set to open at 10,000 feet. The flak would be drawn up to the flares at 10,000 feet.

In the light of 40 flares the A4's would drop down to 200 feet and bomb the ship and be gone. I was confident this could work. CAG approved the plan. Again I asked for volunteers.

On the night of the mission there were many buildups and thunderstorms in the Gulf of Tonkin. We launched and had difficulty tanking because of the turbulence.

The night was black. I was trying to plug into the basket as it gyrated through an arc of five or 6 feet. Lightning flashed in the background.

I said to myself, "Leue, you must be out of your mind. You got a loving wife and six kids at home and this is all your idea."

We went lights out. I dropped down with my wingmen while using my radar to look for the distinct shape of the coastline off of Vinh Harbor.   At that time the A3 leader called and said, "There is a massive thunderstorm over the target. There's no way we can complete this mission."

Thank you Lord.

I directed all aircraft to find other targets of opportunity, then I proceeded to the beach. The weather was so bad we were not able to find any meaningful targets.

After recovering back aboard the ship I debriefed the flight. Although they said nothing before the mission the general consensus of the participants was that we had pushed as hard as we could on this target. It was time to back off before we lost someone. I agreed.

They had brought me to my senses.

CHAPTER TEN

Lieutenant Commander Wendy Rivers

September 10, 1956. I had been Acting Skipper for almost a month, During this period our pilots averaged 30 missions, one a day. The Air Wing had lost two more pilots and aircraft, Lieutenants Junior Grade Shaw of VA-165 flying an A1 and Goodwin of VFP-63 in a RF-8A photo plane. We were physically and mentally tired. Tomorrow we were scheduled to leave Yankee Station for a week of R&R in Cubi Point, the Philippines.

I was designated as strike leader for a JCS Alpha strike on the Ben Thuy port facility. This was the same harbor, near Vihn

VA-153 A4C 313 USS Coral Sea   OJ Greene Photo

where Bill Kraus and I attacked the ship earlier. Now, no ships were in the harbor. Our target would be the docks and port facilities. It was unusual that we would be scheduled against such a heavily defended target, on the last day of an at sea period. I went to see the Operations Officer, Commander Warren O'Neil, with my concerns.

I didn't consider the docks at the Ben Thuy port facility, without a ship in the harbor, to be a significant target. The target was just partially destroyed docks and warehouses. Yet, Ben Thuy, adjacent to Vihn, I knew too well, was defended by hundreds of 85 mm, 57 mm, 37 mm and lesser guns; the 85 mm were radar controlled. Why go there?

Commander O'Neil explained: reconnaissance showed BenThuy was only 40 percent destroyed and the USS Coral Sea had to show at least 60 percent destroyed, for JCS credit. If the weather was okay, we were to go.

The weather report looked marginal; I silently prayed that the weather reconnaissance aircraft would come back with a "no-go"

VA-53 Blue Tails manning aircraft   USS Coral Sea   OJ Greene Photo

report. However, as luck would have it, the reconnaissance pilot reported, "There are breaks in the overcast, it looks like you can make it."

The strike consisted of sixteen A4 Skyhawks, eight from each attack squadron, VA-153 and VA-155. Lieutenant Commander Wendy Rivers, Operations Officer of VA-155, would lead the VA-155 strike aircraft. Another VA-155 division of four A4Es, led by Commander Jim Morin, CO of VA-155, would perform the Iron Hand, or anti-SAM mission. Eight   F8 Crusader fighters were assigned for MIG CAP, and two Electronic Counter Measures aircraft for MIG alerts. Each A4 attack aircraft was loaded with two, one thousand pound bombs, fused .25 seconds delay.

I briefed the mission to proceed to the target at 20,000 feet, with a dive from that altitude. VA-153 would dive first, followed by VA-155.

From experience, I knew the Vietnamese radar controlled 85mm guns would zero in on our roll-in point, the point where we started our dives. I briefed a steep dive, sixty degrees, without speed breaks. (We called this the "Harry Thomas, Mach Memorial Dive" in honor of our late Skipper).

I made a special point, "The weather is marginal, this target is not worth the loss of an aircraft or pilot. If I see the target and commence my dive, follow me, whether you have the target in sight or not. Do not tarry at the roll-in point looking for the target, follow me."

Coral Sea's flight deck crews expeditiously catapulted the strike of over thirty aircraft into a sullen broken overcast sky, with multiple cloud layers. Our rendezvous was above the top of the mid-layer clouds, at fifteen thousand feet over the ship.

Once formed, I led the strike west, between cloud layers, toward the Ben Thuy port facility without difficulty. Approaching the target, there were breaks in the lower cloud layers. As I crossed the beach, I caught a glimpse of the docks at Ben Thuy through a break in the clouds.

I called, "Rolling in," rolled on my back, then pulled my A4C's nose down to the target, commencing my steep dive, then rolled upright holding the docks in my sight. All eight VA-153 Skyhawks followed me.

In my dive I heard Lieutenant Commander Rivers transmitted, "I don't have the target!" I called , "Roll in Wendy, Roll in!"

I pickled my bombs on the Ben Thuy docks, pulling hard, six "Gs", coming out of my dive at 1500 feet at over 500 knots.

I heard Wendy's wingman call, "Silver Fox One is hit, I have a good chute."

I stayed low, holding my speed, pulling hard to the left, under the broken overcast. I turned about 160 degrees, searching for Wendy's chute or the crash site.

I directed the rest of my flight out over the water, to orbit until they were needed for RESCAP (Rescue Combat Air Patrol).

About half a mile to the north, in a small rugged valley, I caught sight of the burning wreckage of Wendy's A4. I saw his white chute on the ground close to the crash site.

As I approached Wendy's burning aircraft at 1000 feet altitude, I was greeted by an avalanche of fat red tracers, 57mm flak, arcing over the hills from the vicinity of Vihn.

I switched the flight to guard channel, calling Wendy repeatedly, "Wendy, Wendy, this is Blue Tail One, do you read me?" He was wearing a PRC radio, tuned to guard channel.

I received no reply.

I made repeated passes over the crash site. Each time, I received heavy fire, arcing over the hills from the direction of Vihn. I pressed lower and found, if I stayed very low, below 300-400 feet, the hills to the west toward Vihn shielded me from this deadly fire.

The RESCAP, prop driven AD Sky raiders from VA-165 arrived. I escorted them to the vicinity of the crash site, cautioning them to stay low to avoid the flak.

Commander Morin remained high over the water. I relayed the details of the shoot down and the possibility of rescue to Commander Morin, and he in turn relayed to the ship and to the rescue net.

There was a was requirement that a downed pilot be "in-sight," before a rescue helo would be sent. I had seen Wendy's chute briefly on my very first pass. Later, when I requested helos I was asked, "Is the pilot in sight?" I replied, "Affirmative." I felt Wendy was hiding; it was worth bending the rules to get him back. I believe, everyone involved with the rescue, my flight, the RESCAP pilots and Commander Morin, understood what was up.

There appeared to be troops with mobile guns coming down from the hills to the west on the road from the vicinity of Vinh. I called my flight of A4 Skyhawks back; they and the AD RESCAP strafed the mobile guns and anything else that moved in the vicinity of the crash site. When required, I went out to sea to refuel from a waiting A3 tanker. At those times Bill Kraus, took over.

It took two and a half hours, for two large, "Jolly Green" Air Force rescue helicopters, to arrive from Thailand. Despite cautions, the Jolly Greens flew too near Vihn and were promptly hosed down with heavy anti-aircraft artillery. They quickly retraced their steps, went south, and then approached from the sea. At this point, we again called Wendy repeatedly on guard. There was no answer.

The RESCAP brought the helicopters to the vicinity of the crash site and called repeatedly. There was no sign of Wendy. The Jolly Greens searched for a reasonable time; then departed for Da Nang. I thanked the Jolly Green leader for their courageous efforts.

I made one last pass over Wendy's chute, pulled up my nose, firing a long, "Take that, you bastards," 20-MM volley, toward the Vinh gunners.

I departed for the ship. The Jolly Greens, the RESCAP from VA-165, Bill Kraus and Commander Morin all did their job, but there was no rescue. Thankfully, we lost no more aircraft in the attempt, as was so often the case. At 4.1 hours this would be my longest combat mission.

The USS Coral Sea departed for Cubi Point, the Philippines immediately after recovering this strike. This mission was my last mission as Acting Commanding Officer of VA-153. Commander Ken MacArthur was waiting in Cubi Point to relieve me as Skipper.

(Wendy Rivers remained a captive of the North Vietnamese seven years until released in 1972. After his return, he reported that he was captured immediately upon landing in his chute. He survived seven years of torture and abuse).

CHAPTER ELEVEN

Commander Ken MacArthur

September 11, 1965. When the USS Coral Sea pulled in to Cubi Point, Philippine Islands, Commander Ken MacArthur was waiting for us. He took over command of Attack Squadron 153 without ceremony.

Commander Ken MacArthur was a Naval Academy Graduate, heavy set physically, with no combat experience. He would have a

CDR Ken MacArthur

very different leadership style from Mongilardi, Thomas and myself.

At first it was difficult for me to step back into the Executive Officer's role having been the commanding officer through some very tough times.

Some of the squadron officers, who had just lost two beloved skippers, had trouble adapting to the new Commanding Officer. I told them he was the new CO, so lets move forward. Commander Ken MacArthur proved to be an excellent officer, a good honest man, steady, with a nice sense of humor, and a good aviator. It would take some time, but he became a well respected leader.

Maybe he wasn't a flamboyant, hard charging Pete Mongilardi or Harry Thomas, but he was steady and firm. Under the circumstance of this prolonged, convoluted conflict, his leadership style was probably not far off the mark. I tried my best to be a good Executive Officer by supporting Commander MacArthur and continued to be a hard charging combat leader.

In day combat operations CDR MacArthur learned quickly and became a steady, competent combat leader. I introduced

Commander MacArthur to our night attack tactics, but he never became a strong believer.

My log book shows I flew 26 missions in September and October after Commander McArthur came aboard. Almost half of these missions were at night. None of these missions were significantly outstanding or hair-raising enough that I recall their details. Since Commander MacArthur was Commanding Officer, he immediately took the lead on day combat missions and strikes. He showed courage and good judgment and quickly developed a firm leadership style.

During this period of time the North Vietnamese continued to build revetments for SA-2 missiles. These sites consisted of six to eight circular revetments around a central fire control revetment. The North Vietnamese would move missiles in and out of these sites randomly.

In October, Commander Wesley McDonald, Commander Ken MacArthur and I, were scheduled together to attack a new missile site located northwest of Than Hoa and south east of Hanoi. However, the site proved to be empty with no missiles, just revetments.

The Vue Chau Bridge raid

Several weeks after Commander MacArthur took over as Commanding Officer the JCS began to offer better targets. A major or Alpha strike was planned on the Vue Chau Bridge, northeast of Hanoi on the northeast railroad running out of China. Two carriers, USS Oriskany and USS Coral Sea, were scheduled to strike this bridge the same day. Oriskany was scheduled to hit the bridge first followed by Coral Sea. Because this was such a desirable target all of the squadron Commanding Officers scheduled themselves on the first strike. Commander MacArthur led our squadron. Due to bad weather and poor navigation by CAG the strike never found the target, but returned with tales of many trains and other targets up in the untouched Northeast area.

A follow-on strike was scheduled and this time the Executive Officers would lead. Commander Jim O'Neill of VA 155 was the overall strike leader and I was scheduled to lead VA-153's three divisions of four aircraft.

Commander Jim O'Neill and I planned our route the night before. We decided to proceed at sea until just 15 miles south of China than turn west paralleling China's border until we hit the prominent limestone or karst ridge that paralleled the northeast railroad running south out of China. At this ridge we would turn south east following the railroad tracks to the Vue Chau railroad Bridge.

Blue Tale taxis out of the gear, USS Coral Sea   OJ Greene Photo

This karst ridge was a great landmark because it stood out in an area where everything was flat and looked the same. We needed something like that because our navigation was strictly dead reckoning and map reading.

Since the Oriskany Air Group would be hitting the bridge first, I requested permission to attack targets of opportunity if the Orkiskany Air Group dropped the bridge first. The large strike rendezvoused quickly, navigation to the coast in point went beautifully. We turned inland descending, then proceeded at 500 feet paralleling the border fifteen miles from China. We received several missile warnings, then several surface-to-air missiles passed harmlessly overhead. I was monitoring the chatter on the radio frequency as the Orkiskany Air Group bombed the bridge ahead of us. I heard a call that the bridge was down. I called to confirm and someone came back and said, "Affirmative, the bridge is down."

We were just approaching the karst ridge and the Northeast Railroad coming out of China. There was a broken overcast at about 1500 feet. I could see a mass of railroad trains three or four wide in the sidings in front of me on the northeast railroad coming out of China. What a target! The squadron was spread out to my right in an echelon of divisions expecting to turn left. I called out, "Blue Tales we are turning right, that is turning right." This was a difficult maneuver, at low altitude, turning right into eleven airplanes to my right. They executed it beautifully.

I climbed to 1500 feet continuing my right turn for 270 degrees. The squadron followed as I dove down the railroad tracks toward the mass of trains. I dropped my two 1000 pound bombs in shallow dive on the trains as did the other 11 aircraft of the squadron, 24,000 pounds of bombs in all. We made just one pass and retraced our steps back home to the ship. There was no antiaircraft fire. These trains were supply trains coming out of China. As we departed there was nothing left but a mass of twisted burning wreckage. This was one of the most successful missions of the cruise. We totally surprised them. I never saw a single round of antiaircraft fire.

Lieutenant Junior Grade Dan Dahl, Wingmen

Shortly after this raid we received news that the Coral Sea would finally be returning to the United States. We flew our last day strike mission on October 14, 1965. Lieutenant Terhune of VF-154 flying a F-8D was shot down and rescued.

I had flown night missions the two previous nights so I was not scheduled. I was in the ready room starting to feel more confident about making it through the cruise. Lieutenant Skip Bennett and Lieutenant Junior Grade Dan Dahl were scheduled for the 2200 launch of night armed reconnaissance. The weather called for thunderstorms over the golf of Tonkin and over Vietnam. Skip Bennett came to me and said, "XO I'm really feeling bad, would you take my hop tonight?" Of all our pilots I worried most about Skip Bennett at night. He had been shot down at night and rescued, now it seemed to affect him.

I thought about it for only a second and said, "Sure Skip, no problem, I'll take it." Besides this would give me an even 100 missions for the cruise.

I briefed the mission with Dan Dahl, we launched and refueled

LTJG Dan Dahl receives congratulations for 100 landings from CDR MacArthur

with the A3 tanker. There were big build ups everywhere over the gulf. After tanking I dropped down to 4000 feet my normal altitude when heading for the beach. I told Dan to stay 1000 feet above me at 5000 feet and hold 270 knots and I would call headings. This was our normal tactic. I tried unsuccessfully using several different routes to get around thunderstorms trying to get to Route 1, the major truck route along the coast. I was unsuccessful. I turned south, skirted the thunderstorms and finally penetrated into Vietnam well below the normal truck routes. I went all the away into Laos and came back into Vietnam from west to east finally picking up Route 1 and turning north. We dropped flares and scoured the roads but found no trucks. Finally, we expended our bombs on the road and small bridges. During this entire mission, through terrible build ups and thunderstorms, I was operating with out lights. I happen to glance out during a lightning flash and I saw Dan locked on my wing. I was astounded; how he could fly my wing in that black goo without lights is beyond me. Dan Dahl was some aviator, typical of our young wingmen such as O.J. Greene, Steve Cole, Ivan Keesey and Paul Reyes. I was to find out later that Dan was also a Mensa, that is a certified genius. We became very close friends, years later, long after we had both left the Navy.

Going Home, Finally

The USS Coral Sea pulled into Cubi Point, Philippine Islands, October 15, 1965. Lieutenant Commander Walker Lambert Assistant Operations Officer to Jim Snyder was a big, quiet, and very competent Naval Officer and aviator. His support of Jim Snyder was a large part of what made the operations department of the squadron work smoothly. During the period of time that I was Acting Commanding Officer he functioned as Operations Officer and did an outstanding job. We became very good friends.

After Coral Sea tied up, Walker Lambert and I excitedly went to the Navy exchange to buy presents for our wives and children. I thought it would be a good idea to buy Jane a set of golf clubs so I could teach her the game, then we could play golf together when I came home. Walker also bought several presents for his wife.

We were in uniform with hats, carrying all are our presents. We decided on our way back to the ship to stop by the old Cubi officers club for a beer. Carrying all this gear I pushed the door open with my foot.

"Bong, Bong, Bong!!"

We had our hats on ...the bartender rang the bell. That meant we had to buy drinks for everyone in the bar. The place was jammed with hundreds of the officers from the USS Coral Sea.

Well, we bought hundreds of drinks, maybe more. At $0.15 a drink we could handle it. We also ended up staying all night. I'm sorry to say we got totally smashed.

During this last night of revelry, I saw my old Guided Group Two buddy, Lieutenant Stan Olmsted's name on a plaque hanging over the bar. I contemplated throwing my glass at his plaque as a symbol of friendship. This was not unusual behavior for aviators coming out of Vietnam in the Cubi Club.

(I did not realize that Stan had been shot down and killed. Years later when I was Air Wing Commander on USS Independence, Lieutenant Commander Glenn Simmerly, my Operations officer, told me that the USS Independence strike group had approached the same karst ridge where I had attacked the trains on the Vue Chau raid. They were greeted by a massive volley of radar aimed 85 mm flak the Chinese had moved in., They shot down several aircraft, including Stan Olmsted's F-4 Phantom. Stan's Vietnamese RIO or back-seater, bailed out of Stan's stricken aircraft successfully, was captured, and

later wrote a book about his life and this incident. "Sense Of Duty" by Quang X. Pham.)

After a brief stay in Cubi Point, Philippines the USS Coral Sea headed east at 26 knots.

I frankly told the officers and crew of Attack Squadron One Fifty Three, that the sustained valor demonstrated by them in combat with little or no acclaim from their country, took more courage and dedication than that required of their World War II contemporaries at Midway or Coral Sea. I believe that today.

No Navy Crosses. Just guts!

Our morale was high, the joy of returning to the States overshadowed the stark fact that many of us would be back in combat in six months.

On November 10, 1965. Almost a year from its departure, USS Coral Sea turned into the wind off the coast of central California preparing to launch its Air Wing.

CHAPTER TWELVE

New Squadron

NAS Lemoore, November 1965-May 1966

My aviator's logbook shows 2.2 hours, October 31, 1965, from CVA 43 to NLC (NAS Lemoore). Several hundred miles at sea, all twelve of Light Attack Squadron, VA-153, A4C Skyhawks were catapulted in order. Joining we flew to our home base at Naval Air Station, Lemoore, California. The homecoming was

LT OJ Greene is greeted by his wife Gina, Porterville H.S. band in the background

VA-153 wives painted squadron colors on the on the base A4 display

joyous; Squadron wives and families crowded the ramp at Naval Air Station Lemoore as we taxied in. The Portervillle High School Band was present in full regalia playing wonderful, happy songs for us. Jane, Debbie, Krista, Cathy, Emily, Becky and Paul were all out there. This had to be one of life's happiest moments.

After the happy celebration, hugging and kissing the family, Lieutenant Commander Dick Coleman, a big gregarious ex-Marine, introduced himself, he had orders to our squadron and would be our new Operations Officer. Dick had been busy, he assured me our squadron spaces were ready for the squadron's return.

Jane and Cathy

Jane, Paul and Eric

Cathy, Krista, Emily & Paul

Paul's 3rd Birthday

It would be several days before our crew and equipment would arrive from Alameda. As Executive Officer, my main concern was the readiness of the squadron spaces at Naval Air Station Lemoore. Since Dick Coleman had done my work for me. I relaxed with the family until the squadron returned.

Once the squadron was settled in its spaces, we granted maximum leave to the crew. The squadron was scheduled to deploy back to Vietnam in May 1966, aboard the USS Constellation, CVA-64. This was to be a very rapid and difficult turnaround. The squadron was losing a significant number of its combat trained pilots and enlisted personnel who were transferring to shore duty. Our job now was to safely integrate and train the new people into the squadron in a brief few months.

Lieutenant Commanders Jim Snyder, Operations Officer, and his Assistant, Walker Lambert, both outstanding officers and

Jim Snyder, clowning, Star Ferry

combat pilots, were departing. Each of these officers had over a hundred combat missions, both were steady as a rock, and would be very hard to replace. The squadron Maintenance Officer, Lieutenant Commander Bill Majors, another strong combat aviator, was departing, as were many of the junior officers. Replacing them were Lieutenant Commanders Dick Coleman, Operations Officer, Len Giuliani, Assistant Operations Officer and Danny O'Connell, Maintenance Officer. Danny had been in charge of the USS Coral Sea Carrier Controlled Approach (CCA), early in the cruise. He had requested the Blue Tails after watching us perform night after night in Vietnam. None of these officers had combat experience, but all would prove to be strong officers, fast learners and outstanding combat pilots.

LCDR Commander Dick Coleman took charge of the squadron

spaces. I felt comfortable taking the family south to Los Angeles and San Diego to visit my Uncle Carl and Aunt Hazel Leue and relax. This was a pleasant trip, Carl and Hazel took us to Knott's Berry Farm where we all had a fine time.

Before Jim Snyder left the squadron he accompanied me to Fresno to pick up a pure-bred Black Lab puppy, a Christmas present for son Paul. All puppies are cute and beautiful, but this Black Lab was especially so. We named him Eric, he was Herbie's replacement. We had a fenced backyard, so Jane and I anticipated no problems with the new puppy.

Squadron Re-Training

During this period of time we also said goodbye to Lieutenants Howard Alexander, Ross Underhill, Skip Bennett and Chuck McNeil, These officers were all strong and aggressive in combat

VA-153 Blue Tais over the Sierra

and diligent in their duties. They would be sorely missed.

We received an equally an strong group of officers; Lieutenant Commander Tom Poore, Lieutenants Steve Werlock, Jim Boardman, Jim Harrington and Dave Patz, Lieutenants Junior

Grade Charlie Klopsch, Steve Macaleer, Bill Beyers, Jim Dienstl and Ivy Ivis. All would prove to be strong, courageous and highly motivated officers.

The squadron did some light training in December, but the second week in January we started flying in earnest.   Initially, we operated exclusively out of NAS Lemoore. The last two weeks in January we deployed to NAS Fallon, Nevada for extensive night and day weapons training. My logbook shows almost 40 hours flown in the last three weeks of January 1966.

In February, we returned to NAS Lemoore to emphasize night operations. We set out to teach this new group of aviators our night tactics against trucks.   We used the Chocolate Mount Impact area for these flights.

In late February we went on board our new ship, USS Constellation, for carrier qualifications.   The ship would be deploying with the first A6A Intruder, all weather attack squadron, and with our old A4E friends, VA 155.   Although Constellation was much larger than Coral Sea, to accommodate the new A6A squadron, our squadron would share a ready room with our sister squadron, VA 155.

Our rapid training cycle was reasonably trouble-free. I struggled to adapt to the leadership style of our new Commanding Officer, Commander Ken McArthur. He was more oriented toward the

The best! VA-153 Chief Petty Officers USS Constellation, May 1966

administrative functioning of the squadron than his predecessors, Commanders Mongilardi and Thomas, who were predominately operators.

During weapons training at Fallon Nevada, the Air Wing lost two F4 Phantoms and crews to a senseless mid-air collision. The pilots were apparently showing off, trying to act like Blue Angels.

I also had an incident, while operating from USS Constellation off the coast of Southern California, late in February.

During night in-flight refueling the check valve in my refueling probe stuck open allowing fuel to pour directly into my engine compartment, filling my cockpit with fuel vapor, making it impossible for me to see my instruments or switches. Fortunately, I was able to find the cabin dump switch by feel, clearing the fuel from the cockpit. This same failure had been responsible for several engine fires, explosions and aircraft losses. I diverted to NAS Miramar to have the engine checked.

Back to War

All to soon, in mid-May 1966, we again said our goodbyes to our families, loaded our the squadron gear on trucks, flew to NAS North Island, where our aircraft and gear were put aboard USS Constellation. The USS Constellation and Air Wing Fifteen, headed west toward Vietnam once more.

Chief Petty Officer Turgeon, the squadron's outstanding maintenance chief, came to me and expressed his concern that many of the new enlisted men were now grumbling about our involvement in Vietnam. Obviously, they were being influenced by the growing negative slant the press was giving the war. There was good reason for dissent, the public was presented with an array of conflicting information. The Soviets, the true instigators of the take over of the free government of South Vietnam, sat aloof. The North Vietnamese insurgents had strong support among the world wide Left. Eastern Europe was still solidly

Top: Morrell, Klopsch, Harrington, Dienstl, Macaleer, Wilkins, Coleman , Harrell, Coakley, Desanto, Dill, Bennett, Boardman, Smith. **Bottom:** Keesey, Reyes, Giuliani, O'Connell, MacArthur, Leue, Patz, Werlock, Poore, Kraus

Communist. Much of this propaganda found its way into our own press. Progressives in our country supported North Vietnam.

Given the negative cant of the press, it was difficult for the common man in our country to see why we should send our young to fight in a distant Vietnam. Why were we there so long? Chief Turgeon asked me if I could write something on the subject. I still have the rough notes that I wrote for Commander MacArthur's signature. The piece below was published in our squadron newsletter.

"Why We Fight

There may be chaos in South Vietnam, but stop and think of what has happened in North Vietnam; to the religious of all faiths, the laborer, the intellectual and the common man. There is no chaos -- there is absolute order. Dissent has been silenced. The laborer

cannot strike, the common man cannot demonstrate, the religious cannot worship, the intellectual cannot criticize, the artist cannot create, the state is God. The same can be said of China. This same order is being forced on South Vietnam. It could be forced on us and our children. This is why we fight.

It is an important fight, it is as important as any this country has ever pursued. Attack Squadron 153 has a big role to play. Navy Light Attack squadrons are among the most effective offensive weapon systems now being used in Vietnam. We hit them hard last time and will hit them even harder this time. This newsletter is the first in a series, which will be put out monthly, to keep all Blue Tails and their families informed. The families that support the sailors of this squadron have been our most valuable asset. We thank them all for their prayers and un-wavering support in the past. Finally, remember that this is an extremely important cruise. Our performance depends on the efforts of every man in the squadron. A happy sailor does a good job, families can keep your man happy by writing happy letters and carrying your share of the effort at home cheerfully. Keep them happy.

Thank you,

Commander KV MacArthur"

We deployed on USS Constellation in early June 1966 with high spirits and optimism.

CHAPTER THIRTEEN

USS Constellation CVA-64

Back to War

June, 1966. In many ways we were a brand-new squadron. Surprisingly, we came out of the intense five month training a very strong and motivated squadron. Although relatively inexperienced, our new top leadership: Commander Ken MacArthur, Commanding Officer; Lieutenant Commanders Dick Coleman, Operations; Len Giuliani, Assistant Operations; Danny O'Connell Maintenance; and Tom Poore, Ordnance. All proved to be outstanding aviators and officers. The squadron came together as a cohesive and strong fighting group. We had the best Chief Petty Offers and crew in the fleet. We enjoyed totally reliable, superbly maintained aircraft.

USS Constellation CVA-64

Thoughts about the Future

The USS Constellation operated briefly in the Hawaiian Islands where the air wing and ship were given an operational readiness inspection. We had a brief stay ashore; a group of us played golf and had drinks at the local watering holes.

As we sailed west, my attitude was definitely one of suspense. I was heading into the fifth combat cruise of my life and I knew I was pushing the odds.

I strongly supported our fighting for South Vietnam. I studied and knew well the history of the long struggle for free China, our arming of Mao over the objections of Chang Kai Shek during WW II, and the unhappy result. The same arguments were made in that conflict, "The rebels aren't really Communist, they are just "Agrarian reformers." We know how that came out. I knew this was another in a series of conflicts brought on by the Soviets successful strategy of, "Small Wars of Liberation." The Soviets were the silent muscle behind the flow of weapons and propaganda we faced.

I felt we were losing the fight for the minds of our own people. It was frustrating. I knew we would be fighting with onerous restrictions imposed by, "The Rules of Engagement." I was sure we would be denied attacking the real targets, the Soviet Block ships bringing the weapons which would kill our countrymen in South Vietnam. Could we attack the docks at Haiphong or power plants? Would we be restricted to attacking only designated targets such as petroleum, bridges, trucks, trains and other transportation targets, as in the past, all very heavily defended, with little chance of hurting the enemy significantly?

Because of the proximity of Laos and Cambodia, it was relatively easy for the North Vietnamese to transport Soviet weapons over the passes into these countries. Once in Laos and Cambodia, mostly safe from our airpower, they could be carried to within 40 miles of Saigon.

I had lost so many friends to this point, I long ago mentally pre-expended myself, so fear had been greatly diminished. I knew the odds. I also knew there would not be great acclaim from the nation for our service.

Our losses would be much harder on Jane than myself. She was the one that had to go with the Chaplain to inform the squadron wives and families when we lost pilots. She had done this duty since Harry Thomas was killed on Coral Sea. She told me later, she stopped smoking "Cold Turkey," saying to herself, "Someone has to survive to bring up the children."

Still, I was highly motivated; free people deserve to remain free. I slept well and concentrated on the challenge that lay ahead. I had a wonderful wife and family that loved and supported me. I knew it was important that I stay positive and pass my combat expertise to the younger and less experienced. I went to Mass daily and prepared myself for any eventuality.

Commander Ken McArthur

Commander MacArthur would prove to be a steady squadron commander and competent combat leader. He had a totally different style from the flamboyant Commanders Mongilardi and Thomas, that preceded him. Still, he imposed a confident, solid leadership on the squadron. It became apparent that this type of war was not going to be won in a hurry. His style fit the nature of the conflict. It was apparent to all, that we would have to fight smart to minimize our own exposure and losses to be able to survive. I personally learned much from Commander MacArthur about leadership and administration.

USS Constellation

USS Constellation, affectionately called "the Connie," was a modern Forrestal class carrier with four of the latest steam catapults, a big deck, and excellent lighting. Captain Houser, the Connie's Commanding Officer, was a very personable officer who took unusual interest in his ship's squadrons. Both the ship and squadrons were highly motivated and believed in our capabilities and our mission. Commander Jake Ward, former Skipper of VF-151, our F-4 phantom squadron, was scheduled to relieve Commander Wes

McDonald as Commander Air Wing 15. The air wing had been strengthened by the addition of another F-4 Phantom squadron, VF-161, with Commander Dick Schulte, Commanding, in place of our F8 squadron. Also added, was a new photo reconnaissance squadron flying the very capable RA5C, with Commander Charlie Smith Commanding. This supersonic aircraft had greatly improved photographic and electronic intelligence gathering systems that were married to the USS Constellation's Integrated Operational Intelligence Center, IOIC. Of course, supporting all this technology, was the backbone of the Navy, the highly trained Petty Officers and Chief Petty Officers, with the skills and dedication to make it all work.

Capt Houser

New Weapons

We had some new weapons. First, was the Hughes MK-4 gun pod. This was a rotating 20 mm "Gatling" cannon in a pod, that was carried under our wing. The gun pod could fire 6000 20mm rounds a minute, awesome firepower, but it had reliability problems.

The second weapon was a new larger version of the Bullpup radio controlled missile with a range of 7 miles and a 1000 pound special warhead. It would prove to be a "bridge buster."

Also, our aircraft had been up graded to give us protection against radar control guns and surface-to-air missiles. An electronic track breaker called ALQ-51 was installed in place of one of our 20 MM cannons. This device, made by the Sanders Corporation, confused and disrupted gun and missile control radars. However, we lost one 20MM cannon to make room for this equipment.

The best! VA- 153 Machinist Mates USS Constellation, May 1966

One sister squadron, VA-65, was equipped with the new A6A Intruder. It had a two man crew with a sophisticated radar and computer system that was designed to find and attack targets at night and in all weather. On the down side, the A6A, built before solid state electronics, required a tremendous amount of maintenance. VA-65 took center stage for the limited resources on the ship. This was a big problem for Danny O'Connell, our Maintenance Officer.

I contemplated all these things as the USS Constellation raced towards the Gulf of Tonkin and combat.

Dixie Station

Our first missions were flown on June 15, 1966 in South Vietnam. The ship operated well south in an area called, "Dixie Station." We operated there for one week doing close air support for US Army and Marine troops. These missions were an easy warm up for what was to come when we operated from Yankee Station up north.

Briefing for our first mission, our Flight Surgeon, who had grounded me earlier for walking pneumonia, came in the ready room and said, "XO you can't fly, your grounded." No way was I going to miss this first mission leading our new pilots. I said, "Doc, I'm better, I'm flying." I flew the mission.

The major challenges on Dixie Station were weather and navigation. In the summertime, South Vietnam was subject to monsoon conditions with thunderstorms and massive cloud build-ups over the Gulf of Tonkin.

Yankee Station

After a week on Dixie Station we steamed north to Yankee Station, at approximately 18N Latitude, 108 East Longitude for strikes against North Vietnam. Our first strike was against the Yen Hau ammunition storage. The strike consisted of about sixteen aircraft. The A4 ordinance load was four LAU-3 rocket packs. The LAU-3 consisted of multiple 2.75 inch rockets in a container. They imposed a very high drag on the airplane and were very inaccurate. A terrible ordnance load. I tried to convince CAG to never give us this weapon again. Unfortunately, the Air Wing lost an VF 151 F-4B and crew on this mission.

The following day we were scheduled against the Phuc Trac railroad bridge. An A6A flown by Lieutenant Weber from VA-65 was hit. Lieutenant Weber flew his aircraft over the gulf where he and his navigator Lieutenant Junior Grade Marik ejected. I was listening and proceeded to the site of Weber's ejection to give assistance. His position was close to Hon Mat island off the coast from Vihn. As we approached the site of the ejection my wingman cautioned me, "XO heads-up for the chute at 12 o'clock." There in front of me was a parachute. We zoomed by on either side of the chute. An A4 pilot from our sister carrier, attempting to help in the A6A rescue wandered too close to Hon Mat island and was hit and ejected. I found out later the pilot was my next-door neighbor from Lemoore, LT Hugh McGee. You can never tell who you might run into halfway across the world. Both Lieutenants McGee and Weber were subsequently rescued, but unfortunately Lieutenant Junior Grade Marik was never recovered.

The war was evolving. Our government was slowly authorizing more significant targets. A few airfields and power plants were added to the target list. Attacks on these targets were called "Alpha

Strikes." Stiff opposition in the form of heavy antiaircraft artillery, surface-to-air missiles and possible attacks by MIG aircraft could be expected. Alpha strike groups usually consisted of twenty eight to thirty-two aircraft, broken down into eight or more flak suppressing F-4 fighters, two barrier combat air patrol, (BARCAP), four target combat air patrol (TARCAP) and twelve to sixteen attack aircraft, plus support provided by electronic countermeasures and photo intelligence aircraft.

Commander Chuck Peters

June 1966. Commander Chuck Peters relieved Commander Jim Morin, as Commanding Officer of our sister A4 squadron, VA-155. Chuck Peters, was very a big fellow, somewhat older than the rest of us. He had a friendly face touched by painful experience. Commander Peters was well known among west coast Naval Aviators. He had inadvertently flown his Skyhawk into the water at night, a year or two earlier. He survived by holding on to one of his floating drop tanks until rescued. He spent many months in the hospital, but doggedly returned to flying.

On our first Alpha strike, June 30, 1966, on the Kep airfield near Hanoi, Commander Chuck Peters flew his first mission as Commanding Officer. During his dive on the airfield his aircraft was hit by AAA and caught fire. I heard Commander Peter's wingman report the details as Peter's flew his burning A4E out over

Kep Airfield strike June 30, 1966

CDR Bud Ingley

the Gulf of Tonkin, where he ejected. His wingmen followed him down, and reported that Commander Peter's parachute opened properly, but then descended into the water and sank. Possibly, Chuck Peters was wounded or hurt in the ejection. We will never know.

Shortly afterward, Commander Bud Ingley was ordered into VA-155 as Commanding Officer.

Commander Bud Ingley was very junior because of the recent heavy losses in Navy A4 squadrons. When he came aboard, I briefed him on my thoughts and experiences concerning our combat including night attacks on trucks. In the past, VA 155 would have little to do with Blue Tail low level night tactics against trucks. Bud Ingley was to become an enthusiastic ally, embracing aggressive night tactics against trucks.

LT Charlie Klospch, the Bullpup missile

During the day, the majority of our targets were against the transportation system infrastructure such as road and railroad bridges, fuel and oil storage facilities, radar and gun sites, barges and canals and the like. Each pilot flew an average of one mission a day. Our flight schedules were well known to the North Vietnamese, so it was important to achieve some surprise by changing tactics, diving from unexpected directions, sometimes from out of the sun or by splitting the attack force and diving from multiple directions simultaneously.

We devised a novel tactic using the new big Bullpup missile. At seven miles from the target we would break the flight of four into a tail chase formation, then fly on a tangent about 6 miles from the target. On command, all four aircraft would roll toward the target, thus putting each aircraft abeam as they closed the target. At four miles, on command, each pilot launched their missile at the target, in sequence.

The effect of several one thousand pound Bullpup warhead missiles hitting a bridge or other targets broad side was devastating. Dick Coleman, Len Giuliani, Riley Harold and I first used this tactic effectively on the famous Than Hoa Bridge. Flak sites near bridges were usually located off either end of the bridge, where gunners knew we usually pulled out of our dive bombing runs parallel to the bridge. With our Bullpup tactic, we attacked the bridge broadside avoiding most of the flak sites.

We used a modification of this tactic on the large Ha Thon

Charlie Klopsch's big Bullpup hit on the Ha Thon Bridge

railroad bridge, north of Vihn. The flight consisted of four A4 bombers, two Bullpup shooters and several F4 fighter flak suppressors.

We planned the attack to have the bombers roll-in just as our missiles were hitting the bridge.

Ensign Charlie Klospsch expertly guided his Bullpup missile to

LT Charlie Klospch

hit the steel girder railroad bridge broadside, twisting it like a pretzel and dropping it into the river. My own missile went out of control and flew through the fighters formation, who mistook it for a Russian SA-2, giving them quite a scare.

Charlie received the Distinguished Flying Cross for this mission. (This picture of

Charlie's twisted Ha Thon bridge was prominent in the NAS Lemoore, VA 125, ready room for many years. It disappeared from the VA-125 Ready Room with the advent of the FA-18, when the emphasis shifted to "F" for fighter. A pity).

Later that night Lieutenant Commander Len Giuliani attacked the trucks we knew would be stacked up north and south of the damaged bridge. Len's flight was met by a thunderous flak barrage and he, using good judgment, went elsewhere. We did not fight heavy flak at night.

Alpha Strikes Nam Dinh

Later, we had two major Alpha strikes on Nam Dinh, thirty miles southeast of Hanoi, on the same day. Each strike consisted of over 30 aircraft, including the fighters, flak suppressors, jammers, bombers and Bullpup missile shooters. The Big Bullpup was the star of these strikes. On one of these missions I carried two big Bullpup's and was able to hit and knock down a bridge with each. There was excellent flak suppression and although there was significant antiaircraft fire, we lost no aircraft. The air wing dropped five or six bridges in Nam Dinh that day.

Night Attack, North Vietnamese Trucks

In the Gulf of Tonkin, the weapons of war continued to flow past the United States Navy on a daily basis, in Soviet bloc ships. These weapons were then offloaded in the port of Haiphong. We were forbidden to attack the Soviet ships or the docks at Haiphong. These weapons were loaded on trucks which traveled south, at night, on Route 1 then across Vietnam on Route 116, over Maguia and Bartholomew passes into Laos, where they were mostly immune to our air power. From there they flowed safely through Cambodia to within 40 miles of Saigon. The Navy's best option to stop these weapons was to destroy the trucks on Route 1 and Route 116 at night.

Earlier, while in Lemoore, I enthusiastically related the VA-153 night attack philosophy and its success, to my next door neighbor, Lieutenant Commander Jude Lahr. Jude was Operations officer of another A4 squadron. He invited me to brief his squadron, which was about to deploy to Vietnam for the first time. In this briefing, I described in detail our low level tactics, the methods of finding and killing trucks.

I passed on Harry Thomas's valuable tactics to this sister squadron. I felt the briefing went well. Years later, Jude told me after the briefing and I left their ready room his Commanding Officer locked the ready room door, went to the front and stated, "Gentlemen, what you heard here today, ... forget it!"

This attitude was probably typical of Navy squadrons of the time. This incident showed the great disparity of opinions on tactics and risks that existed in Naval attack squadrons. Jude Lahr's Commanding Officer was obviously very competent and well thought of. He was later promoted to Admiral.

July 11, 1966. Big Truck Kill. Lieutenant Commander George Wilkins.

One memorable mission, flown on the night of July 11, 1966 clearly shows the potential and the risks of our tactics.

Usually, on night missions each squadron was given an exclusive route or sector to work in looking for trucks. My personal favorite sector was Route 1 in the area west of Hon Me Island, along Brandon Bay between Vihn and Than Hoa. Most North Vietnamese trucks traversed this section of Route 1 with lights out on their way to Laos.

On this mission, my wingman, Ensign Riley Harrell and I were briefing when we were informed that Commander Bud Ingley of VA-155 and his wingmen were also scheduled into the same area. Rather than make a fuss about the scheduling foul-up, CDR

Ingley and I agreed to operate on the same radio frequency and keep each other informed of our positions and altitudes. VA-155 was flying the newer A4E, with better fuel specifics and more ordinance stations than our A4C. They did not require in-flight refueling and would get to the attack area first.

This night was pure black, broken clouds, no moon and no horizon. I rendezvoused with the tanker sporting a green recognition light at 5000 feet. Riley joined. We plugged the tanker in order and topped off our fuel. I then turned to 320 degrees for Hon Me Island. I descended to 4000 feet, leaving Riley at 5000 feet, as briefed. I went lights out approaching the beach.

Glowing on my radar, I could see Hon Me Island ahead and slightly right. I transmitted, "Power House One, Heading 330," to Riley, my wingman.

Bud Ingley called, "Powerhouse One, this is Silver Fox One, I have trucks on Route 116."

I replied, "Power House will be right there to help you." I pushed my throttle to 100%.

My radar shows the coastline three miles ahead.

Suddenly, ahead to my right, hundreds of shafts of bursting flak erupted. Red, orange and green balls of fire arched through the clouds, lighting up the black night like daylight, like a scene from Walt Disney's Fantasia!

I thought, "Bud Ingley must be over Than Hoa, not Route 116. Than Hoa's guns are having a field day"

Bud Ingley's frantic voice, strained, pulling Gees, "This can't be Route 116!!"

Crossing the coast, another surprise. Below me, I can see a sold line of truck lights winding for miles heading south on Route 1. I can't believe my eyes.

I thought, "North Vietnamese trucks never use lights when they know we were are in the area? Did the noise of all those guns obscure their 'lights out' signal?"

I call, "Silver Fox One, this Powerhouse One, I have miles of trucks with their lights on just below me on Route One"

Now I am over the line of truck lights at 4000 feet.

I call, "Power House One, rolling in south on the truck lights, no flares," I roll left, pulling and diving south. The "G" builds, my heart races.

I turn on my gun-sight, arm my MK-4 gun pod. I accelerate rapidly in a shallow dive into the blackness, 800 feet, now! Squeeze...nothing. My damned MK-4 gun pod is jammed!.

At 450 knots I switch to my internal 20mm, it roars, trucks ahead burst into flames. I continue firing fascinated by my hits, … I'm low!, stick in my lap, I pull out just above the burning trucks.

Whew!

"This is Power House One, I'm off, Powerhouse Two, you're cleared in. Make your dive to the north, hit the trucks on the south end of the convoy," I pull up steeply climbing in a left orbit.

Riley; "Rog, this is Blue Tail Two, I have the burning trucks. I'm rolling in North."

Zooming to 5000 feet I circle left. I see Riley's 20mm tracers knife through the night, lighting fires to the south. A large blast indicates Riley dropped one of his 250 pound "Snake-Eye" retarded bombs.

"Silver Fox One, we have many trucks on Route 1, we need help. Look for the fires, "

Riley, "Powerhouse Two, Off."

"Good hits Two, One's In," I call, rolling in going North, trying to do as well as Riley with my 250 pound Snake-Eyes. I level at 500 feet. I "pickle" two Snake Eye on the north end of the convoy. Pulling up left looking over my shoulder I see more trucks burning behind me. Now we have many trucks burning at each end of the two mile convoy.

"Power House this is Silver Fox One and Two, overhead, six thousand, ready for action." Bud Ingley announces he and his wingman are on the scene.

"Silver Fox One, you are cleared in, make your runs to the north"

I see an almost solid tracer stream from Bud Ingley's Mk4 gun pod, it ignites truck after truck between our fires. His wingman follows and continues the carnage. The four of us keep up this routine.

In order, Riley and I drop a total of twelve, 250 pound Snake Eye retarded bombs and expend our 20mm ammunition. Bud Ingley and his wingman each fire 500 rounds from their Mk4 gun pods and drop twelve, 250 pound bombs from their MBR racks.

After each run the smoke builds. Hundreds of trucks are burning and exploding in the convoy. In a period of 10 to 15 minutes, Route 1 is on fire with miles of burning trucks. On my final run there is so much smoke, it is difficult for me to see which trucks are destroyed or damaged and which are not.

I announce "Ammo minus." With 4000 pounds of JP5 indicating on the gauge I call, "Bingo" and turn toward the ship.

Climbing into the black night, the flames still glowing in my rear view mirrors, I head for USS Constellation with great satisfaction. I'm sure undamaged trucks remain trapped in the wreckage of the convoy. I call the USS Constellation, "Mustang, this is Power House One, many trucks burning, Lat 19-38 Long 105-48, still many good targets, recommend more strikes."

I knew our outstanding squadron Maintenance Officer, Lieutenant Commander George Wilkins, a skillful night attack pilot and his wingman were scheduled on the 0200 Launch. I passed small talk with George in the ready room, just before launch. We were both excited about the prospect of meeting our wives in three weeks in Hong Kong.

LCDR George Wilkins receives award

Riley and I landed aboard. In the ready room, Bud Ingley, his wingman, Riley and I enthusiastically shared our views of this wild and successful mission with our squadron mates.

In the midst of our levity the Squadron Duty Officer received a call from Strike Control. The Duty Officer turned to me, looking ashen, "XO, Strike reports Lieutenant Patz, George Wilkins' wingman, said George went in attacking the trucks on Route 1. He observed a long ball of fire, obviously George's aircraft. After many calls on guard there was no response, no beeper, no chance of survival"

I thought, "My God. Is losing George Wilkins, such a fine naval officer and friend, worth burning some lousy trucks? No, those trucks carried thousands of weapons that would never kill our brothers fighting in the south. George died for them"

C'est la guerre.

CHAPTER FOURTEEN

Patrol Torpedo Boats (PTs)

Patrol torpedo boats or PTs figure heavily in the lore of the "Tonkin Gulf Resolution." On August 2, 1964 the destroyer USS Maddox was attacked in broad daylight, by North Vietnamese

Patrol Torpedo Boat (PT)

PT's in the Gulf of Tonkin. Two days later the destroyers USS Maddox and USS Turner Joy were again attacked at night.

In his book, "In Love and War," the late Vice Admiral Stockdale describes searching for these PT Boats on the night of August 4, 1964. On this flight he mistakenly fired a Sidewinder missile at one of the destroyers, then narrowly missed flying into the water. He saw no PT boats on this pitch-black night, then concluded there were no PTs and that the Maddox and Turner Joy were not under attack.

After this second attack, the President ordered the first airstrikes into North Vietnam. Stockdale concluded we had started the war through a hoax, there were no PTs. He was shot down shortly after the PT incidents and spent seven terrible years as a prisoner of war in the "Hanoi Hilton." He received the Congressional Medal of Honor for his conduct during his capture. His book, written after his release, stated his belief there were no PT boats on the night of August 4, 1964. This statement was seized on by many campus academics and ant-Vietnam types. He became a favorite on the lecture tour.

In my view, the wild melee he described was as much a result of his own inexperience in night work as anything else. He was a day fighter pilot flying an F8 fighter, un-trained in night attack.

LCDR Dick Coleman

Regardless, the primary reason the United States went to war in Southeast Asia had nothing to do with PTs. We had assured the South Vietnamese we would protect them against the Communist insurgency. We went to war for the freedom of the South Vietnamese people, which we had sworn to support.

The insurgency to overthrow the South Vietnamese government began years before the 1964 PT incidents.

VA-153's involvement with North Vietnamese PTs took place in August and September 1966. Both of these incidences revolved around Lieutenant Commander Dick Coleman our squadron Operations officer.

August 1966. **First PT Blood.**   Lieutenant Commander Coleman was in the intelligence debriefing spaces looking for good targets, when he heard that two North Vietnamese patrol torpedo boats had been spotted leaving Haiphong harbor. They were reportedly heading for our northern Search and Rescue (SAR) destroyer at high speed.

LCDR Len Giuliani

Dick ran toward the ready room pell-mell with his briefing cards trying to be the first to launch. He was a big man and he hit his head on a hatch coaming, gashing it open, and knocking himself down. His roommate, Len Giuliani, happened upon the bloody scene. Len determined that Dick would live, grabbed Dick Coleman's kneeboard briefing cards and rushed to the ready room to take Dick Coleman's flight. He didn't know what the target was.

Len Giuliani's manned Dick Coleman's aircraft, which was loaded with six Mark 82 500 lb bombs, his wingman, Lieutenant Gary Starbird, had eight 5 inch Zuni rockets. After Giuliani started his aircraft a crewman handed Len a paper with coordinates and no other info. Len looked up at the Air Boss pointing to the paper with a "what the?" hand signal. Now what? Both he and Gary Starbird were quickly taxied to the catapult and launched. Len was not really sure of what the target was and what were their orders. They switched to strike control after launch. Strike vectored them at max speed north west.

Soon they spotted three distinct wakes coming from the direction of Haiphong harbor at very high-speed, heading directly for the SAR destroyer.

Giuliani and Starbird intercepted the wakes, identified them as PTs, about 10 miles from the SAR destroyer. Flying through the 37MM fire from the PT's guns Giuliani's first pass bracketed the lead PT boat with two 500 lbs bombs, severely damaging it. Gary Starbird followed up by hitting the lead PT in the screws with two Zuni rockets. Great hits!

They made multiple runs, succeeding in stopping all three PT boats, leaving them dead in the water and sinking. Len recalls that about 20 North Vietnamese survivors were picked up after the attack and we received excellent intelligence from these captives. Both LCDR Giuliani and LT Gary Starbird were recommended for and received Distinguished Flying Crosses for this outstanding mission.

Of course, Dick Coleman claimed Giuliani stole his DFC.

September 11, 1966. This was the date of my involvement with North Vietnamese PTs. My Aviator's Log Book shows: Lat 20-56 N, Long 107-05E. Flight code1T1, Flight time 1.8 (should be 2.8), Catapult 1, Arrested landing 1, Remarks: 2 Bullpup, PT Boats.

On this morning, my wingman, Lieutenant Commander Bill Coakley and I were in the ready room briefing for an armed reconnaissance mission. During our briefing, Dick Coleman returning from an early armed reconnaissance mission burst into the ready room excitedly proclaiming that he and his wingmen had just discovered several, Swatow class, motor torpedo boats (PTs) hiding in a cove of a karst island east of Haiphong.

This was a major discovery. This class of Chinese PT boat carried torpedoes capable of sinking any Navy ship in the Gulf of Tonkin. Dick Coleman described the PT's, moored close alongside the sheer vertical cliffs of a karst island, hiding under camouflaged netting. He said, "XO, we just found the PTs just by chance. There are so many similar small islands up there, we may never find them again."

I said, half joking, "Dick, why didn't you attack them?"

Coleman reported the discovery of the PT's to the ship's Captain and Air Wing Commander. An immediate strike was ordered.

The Commanding Officer of the A6A Intruder squadron was designated as the strike leader. The strike composition was: eight A6A aircraft, eight F4 Phantom fighters and eight A4s, four each from VA-155 and VA-153.

I was scheduled to lead VA-153's four A4's. I asked Dick Coleman, "Do you want to lead our squadron aircraft? You found the PTs?" He declined, he said he would prefer to go as my section leader. Dick Coleman and his wingman were scheduled to carry six 500 pound bombs. My aircraft was loaded with two VT (influence) fused Bullpup missiles. The VT fuse was designed to explode the missile when it was 50 feet in the air above a target. Bill Coakley, my wingmen, carried a Mark 4 gun pod. We launched, rendezvoused overhead the ship and departed toward the karst islands, one hundred eighty miles north.

We arrived at the approximate location of the PTs. Nothing could be seen, there was a solid cloud layer below. The A6A strike leader circled and made no move to send anyone through the overcast to look for the PT's. Apparently, the A6A bombardier/ navigators were looking for the PT's on their radars. I was quite sure they would never see the PT's on radar; the PTs were reported moored close alongside the karst islands vertical cliffs.

After minutes of circling by the entire strike, with no apparent action from the strike leader, I saw a small break in the clouds below.

I motioned with my hand to Bill Coakley my wingmen, "Come with me." Without saying a word, I rolled on my back and dove through the hole in the clouds below. Apparently, Dick Coleman and his wingman missed my signal.

Bill Coakley and I descended low over the water into the mist below.

We slowed down poking along examining each small karst island as it came into view. It was foggy and hazy, visibility was very poor. The black karst islands loomed out of the fog, rising ominously, vertically, hundreds of feet up into the low overcast. It was eerie.

To see better, I slowed to 250 knots and descended to 200 feet over the water. We poked into coves, nooks and crannies. Coakley stepped up on my wing.

Suddenly, four Swatow PTs, covered in camouflage netting appeared out of the fog, just as Dick Coleman had described them, hiding in a U shaped karst island. The "U" of the cove was open to the north.

They were on our right, two were moored against the east side of the cove with two more less than a quarter of a mile to the west.

We glided past going east. I held my breath, we were so close. They did not shoot. I watched their 37mm gun mounts for movement. None.

I thought, "Should I call our strike aircraft down? No. There was no room for all those aircraft to attack in this low overcast and fog. "

As I passed the PTs, I slowly dropped my wing to port, acting as if I hadn't seen them. I kept them in sight, looking over my left shoulder. I started an easy climb to about 500 feet altitude.

"Now what ? The Bullpup missile requires that I dive at the target with no jinking. Each of the PTs has 37mm anti-aircraft guns fore and aft. That's eight guns, there may be more guns in the hills.

We have Coakley's gun pod, my VT Bullpup won't help until the second run.

This will be: 'The shoot out at OK Corral.' Eye ball to Eye Ball.

I am losing site of the PTs...   Nuts! I 'll attack!!"

Throttle 100%. Hard port turn. I wrapped it up in a steep bank back toward the eastern PT's, leveling my wings in a shallow dive. I touched the firing button on the stick. My starboard Bullpup blasts off with a roar.

Immediately, fat orange tracers arc toward us from the PTs and the guns in the hills above.

To my dismay, my missile veers wildly right.

"Great! We are committed and my missile is going crazy."

Instinctively, I hold full left command and accelerate past 450

37 MM gun mounts on Swatow Class Motor Torpedo Boats

knots through the crisscrossing orange tracers.

Time seems to stand still as I hold full left command.... tracers spaying on both sides in my peripheral vision.

The missile veers sharply back left toward the PT's. Coakley's gun pod roars.

For frozen seconds, we press on though the tracers, holding full left command, the missile veers back toward the eastern PT.

Waco!!!

A satisfying explosion of black and red envelops the PTs bridge, a strange red cloud of smoke bellows skyward from the shattered PT. (Flares?)

Cove at 20-56 N, 107-05, Google Earth

"Never make two runs." "

The karst cliff looms ahead, 450 knots. I pull hard left in an almost vertical bank under a hail of 37 mm fire. Coakley hanging tight on my right wing.

"Now my blood is up, I know I'll violate the second cardinal rule,

I continue north for a mile, climbing, then make a steep port turn, level my wings, missile "Arm." I launch the port missile with a roar. This missile flies strait and true. Minor commands hold the flare between the two western PTs.

We dive towards the western PTs, ...orange balls of fire in my peripheral vision fight for my attention, ...flare on the target, ...hold the flare on the target, ...an eternity, ...,3,2,1 seconds.

Waco!!! A red and black ball of fire explodes between the two western PTs moored side by side. Both PTs erupt with great clouds of red smoke.

Pulling hard left, I zoom out of range of the 37mm.
Relaxing I called the strike leader orbiting above, "This is Powerhouse 2, we have the four PTs." The strike leader responds, "What is your position?"

With great satisfaction I reply, "Look for the smoke." Three of the four PT's are burning fiercely, black smoke is rising to several thousand feet. The heat is dissipating the overcast above.

I discovered the PT's and started the fight, I take over the mission from the A6A leader. I direct each division of A4s and A6As, when and where to dive. In 15 minutes, all four PT's are sunk or beached, most of the flak sites on the karst are put out of action.

We are fortunate no one is hit. The North Vietnamese Navy gunners put up a very spirited fight. During the fight, I witnessed one PT gun crew continue firing even as their ship was burning and sinking. I felt admiration for this courage.

The USS Constellation sent another strike to be sure none of the beached PTs would ever sail again. Commander MacArthur lead this strike. I remained and orbit high over the PTs, refueling in-flight from a tanker, then guided Commander MacArthur's strike to the site and assisted in the second attack.

At the completion of this strike, the hulks of two PTs can be seen below the surface in the cove. The other two are beached and mangled almost beyond recognition, having sustained multiple bomb hits.

LCDR Bill Coakley

After landing back aboard Constellation there is great jubilation. Significant targets like the PTs are few and far between, sinking all, with no losses is a shot in the arm.

There is one negative aspect. We had up-staged the A6A strike leader and the vaunted A6A squadron. There is great competition among squadrons. We had bruised a significant amount of professional pride.

CHAPTER FIFTEEN

Rest and Recreation, R&R

Looking at the notes I made in my little green back-pocket notebook. It reminded me that our schedule was roughly three to four weeks of intense eighteen hour days at sea, flying strikes against Vietnam. Then, the ship would sail to Cubi Point/Subic Bay, Philippines, Hong Kong or Yokosuka, Japan, for four or five days of unwinding. In Subic Bay, Philippines, our most frequent destination, the major recreation was golf.

Subic Bay Golf. We played in a standard foursome, made up of Danny O'Connell, Len Giuliani, Dick Coleman and myself. Len Giuliani and Dick Coleman were the better golfers of the group and were very competitive. I recall an incident that took place during one of our games at Subic Bay.

Cubi Point and Subic Bay, Philippines

As usual, it was a hot humid day. We were teeing off on the ninth hole, which ended at the clubhouse. Dick Coleman went first and hooked his drive into the jungle. We all had Filipino caddies. They would go into the jungle and retrieve the ball with their toes.

Giuliani, Danny O'Connell and I teed off next. We hit our drives in the fairway. Giuliani and Coleman were tied at this point. Giuliani was happy because Dick Coleman obviously would lose a stroke by going out of bounds into the jungle. As we went by the spot where Coleman's ball went into the jungle, he was standing well out in the fairway next to his ball with an innocent expression that said, "This is where I found it ."

This irritated Len Giuliani, because Coleman was acting as if his ball didn't go out of bounds. After the hole, we stopped in the restaurant to get a hamburger and drink before playing the last nine holes. We all ordered. Giuliani and Coleman ordered Gin and Tonics. Dick Coleman excused himself to go to the head, whereupon Len Giuliani called the waiter back and said, "Put my gin in his drink," pointing to Dick Coleman as he left. When Coleman came back, he quickly finished his drink and said, "Boy, that was good, I'll have another." Len Giuliani winked at the waiter.

When we played the back nine, Dick Coleman could hardly hit the ball, having had four gin and tonics. No one said a word. Len beat Coleman by many strokes. He didn't tell Dick Coleman about it until after we were back in combat. We were very competitive about everything.

It was very rainy in the Philippines during the monsoon season. After being rained-out a number of times, our foursome agreed next time in port we would continue to play no matter what the weather. Well, the next time we played it grew progressively worse until we were playing in a driving down-pour. Finally, Danny O'Connell declared, "You guys are out of your minds, I'm soaked, I'll see you in the bar.

Giuliani, Coleman and I yelled, "Quitter! Quitter," and kept playing as the down pour increased. We were putting on the seventeenth green. The down pour kept washing Coleman's golf ball off of the green. Dick Coleman finally said, "You guys are nuts!" He picked up his ball and stomped off.

Giulliani and I called, "Quitter, quitter," and kept playing. I took eighteen puts. Giuliani only took fourteen.

We never let Coleman and O'Connell forget.

Hong Kong

When in Hong Kong the squadron always took a room at the Hong Kong Hilton. We called this room our "Admin." It was a place where squadron pilots could take their packages and purchases or relax and have a drink. Our Admin was on the 18th floor overlooking the swimming pool at ground level.

Several of the squadron pilots bought radio controlled toys and boats for their children as Christmas gifts. They tried them out in the swimming pool and of course some of their wise-guy

Star Ferry running between Kowloon and Hong Kong

Hong Kong Hilton

buddies dropped water balloons on their boats from the 18th floor.

Phantom   Santa. Shopping in Hong Kong I found a toy airplane that flew around in a circle. You could land it on a little carrier. I bought one for my son Paul and showed it to Danny O'Connell. He got excited and said he'd like one for his kids. Would I buy him one? I said I would, I bought it and put it away. When we were back at sea he ask me, "Skipper, did you buy the carrier landing toy for me? I said, "Danny, I'm sorry I forgot." Of course, this made him mad. I waited until the ship returned home from the cruise before Christmas. Jane and I wrapped Danny's toy and put it on his doorstep, rang his bell and drove away.

It had a card that said, "From the Phantom Santa."

Wives Visit

Since we were gone from our families for over eight months on

Baguio PI

this cruise, Nora O'Connell, Ellen Dill, Peggy Wilkins and Jane planned to fly out and meet us during the October in-port period where the ship planned to be in the Philippines and Hong Kong back to back. Unfortunately, George Wilkins was killed just before this event and it fell to Jane to inform Peggy Wilkins. Jane was a trooper, she did an outstanding job of fulfilling the job of the skipper's wife for two years. If this bothered her, she never showed it.

Jane and I spent a very pleasant four days together in Manila, Subic Bay and Baguio, a resort in the Philippine mountains north of Subic Bay that has a climate very much like the Sierras. (I kept her away from the zoo scene at the Fleet Aviator's Bar in Cubi)

We wined and dined the girls on Philippine fare such as lumpia, champagne and San Miguel Beer. The ship then sailed directly to

Hong Kong from Subic Bay, so Jane and the other wives flew and were waiting at the Hong Kong Hilton when we arrived. Here we showed them the fabulous shopping of the British China Fleet Club, the Hong Kong tailors, Kowhoo Shoe, the thousands of bustling shops, the Star Ferry and the

Dan & Nora O'Connell, Jane & Dave Leue', Walt Dill, Hong Kong

opulent hotels. We dined at great places such as Jimmy's Kitchen in Kowloon with the world's greatest pea soup. (I am now looking at a Jimmy's Kitchen Creamer that Jane put in her purse as a souvenir).

Then, it was back to reality...war.

CHAPTER SIXTEEN

Commanding Officer

I had expected to relieve Commander MacArthur sometime in July, however, due to the tempo of combat operations the Change of Command was delayed until the first week in September, 1966, when the ship was scheduled to be in Hong Kong.

CDR Dave Leue' and XO, CDR Tom Woolcock

Everybody loved the British colony of Hong Kong as a Liberty port. Everything was inexpensive, suits, hi-fi equipment, sewing machines, you name it. It was a bustling, fascinating, fun place. The squadron planned to have a going away party in Kowloon for Commander MacArthur two days before the Change of Command.

Commander McArthur was quite a drinker, so we thought it best if we had his party two nights before the Change of  Command, to be sure he would show up. Several of us took the Star Ferry from Hong Kong Island to Kowloon to select a going away present for Commander MacArthur.

We selected a rattan bar, hired some coulees to take it down to the waterfront where we dickered with several junks to haul it to the Fleet Landing in Hong Kong. This was a fun adventure; there were three generations living on the junk we selected; Grandma and Grandpa, Mom and Dad, many children and grandchildren. It was a happy family. There were thousands of these junks in Hong Kong harbor. They were mostly motorized junks that earned their living by loading and unloading the hundreds of ships that visited Hong Kong yearly. (No Union labor)

September 3, 1966. The going away party in Kowloon was a great success. I returned to the ship that night to prepare for the change of command. It was to take place on the hangar deck of the USS Constellation. I asked Captain Houser, Commanding Officer of the Constellation to be the speaker. Commander Woolcock had the crew arrange two of our airplanes on either side of a raised platform and podium on the hangar deck with several hundred chairs for the guests. All was in readiness for the big day. The event was scheduled for 10 AM so the crew would not miss noon Liberty. I had arranged for a party at the Ambassador Hotel in Kowloon at 1300 that afternoon.

On the day of the change of command I was up early for breakfast. I noticed that Ken McArthur was not aboard. I donned my dress whites with sword and metals then went

CDR Mc Arthur, CDR Leue   Change of Command Hong Kong

below to the hangar deck to check the arrangements. Generally, the crew falls in at least 45 minutes before the scheduled time for this type of event, so at about 0915 they began falling in.

Still, no Commander Ken MacArthur. Commander Woolcock told the crew to fallout and standby, there had been a delay. We had an announcement passed over the ship's PA system, the One -MC. Ten o'clock came and went, still no Commander Ken MacArthur. At about 1100 the Officer of the Deck on the Quarterdeck called and said Commander MacArthur was on the ship to shore phone. I took the phone and the Skipper said, "Dave, I can't get back to the ship, the weather is just too bad and the seas are too rough." I said, "Skipper, everyone else is back aboard and we are waiting for you." After a pause he said, "I'll be there as soon as I can."

About a half an hour later a sampan came alongside and he climbed aboard. I helped the Skipper up to his cabin. He was still feeling the effects of Liberty. I helped him dress in his whites with his sword, etc. We had an announcement passed over the One-MC that the Change of Command would commence at noon.

Somehow we made it through the change of command. It wasn't pretty, but after two tries and a year and a half, I was Commanding Officer of Attack Squadron 153. I still have a treasured note from Vice Admiral Reedy, Commander Task Force 77. It's written on the back of my Change of Command notice in the Admiral's longhand.

I was overjoyed. Someone up there actually noticed and appreciated the risks the squadron took in the black of night, burning trucks. For me, this was better than receiving the Navy Cross.

The party at the Ambassador Hotel in Kowloon had to be canceled; they were unwilling to re-schedule. I announced over the One-MC there would be a party at the Hilton at 1600 (4PM).

I had no way of knowing whether the Hilton could actually put on the party. My next task was to quickly get out of my whites and change into civilian clothes and catch the first officer's

Hong Kong Harbor

motorboat ashore. I went directly to the Hilton and asked, "Could they put on a party for 400 people at 1600 (4PM), with open bar and heavy hors d'oeuvres?"

They didn't blink, they put on a terrific party. When it was time to pay for the party, I pulled out my checkbook... you guessed it, I had used my last check.

I asked if they had a counter check. They produced a blank check. I wrote, "Bank of America" with the appropriate numbers and sum. They took the check without batting an eye. The Chinese are businessmen!

I was Skipper finally. The following day, USS Constellation sailed back toward the Gulf of Tonkin and the unknown.

CHAPTER SEVENTEEN

The Blue Tails, Chief Turgeon, and the MOPIX

September 1966. My first month as skipper. The squadron flew over one thousand hours in combat. A record. We hit major targets in Ninh Binh, Than Hoa, Pho Can and Yen Xa. Our pilots knocked down a series of bridges using the big Bullpup missile

Chief Petty Officer Turgeon

and emphasized night work against trucks.

The quiet strength of the Blue Tails was embodied in its senior enlisted, the Chief Petty Officers. Typical of our CPOs was our Senior Maintenance Chief, Aviation Machinist Mate Turgeon. He had come up through the ranks with years in carrier squadrons. He was quiet, determined and strong. Routinely he worked eighteen hour days ensuring our A4C aircraft were maintained in superb flying condition. The squadron never had an aviation accident of any sort especially one caused by a mechanical malfunction. No task was beyond Chief Turgeon's ability to give the squadron the most reliable and capable aircraft. An incident took place in the midst of our heavy combat that illustrates his amazing talent and dedication.

In Korea, flying the Corsair and the Panther, we had a 16 mm gun movie camera mounted in our fighter's wing that would take gun camera pictures every time the pilot pulled the trigger or hit the bomb release. For whatever reason, these cameras disappeared from jet aircraft in Vietnam. Our A4C and A4E Skyhawks had no gun cameras. Wanting pictures of Vietnam combat, the Navy installed a jury-rigged 16 MM camera in the outer right wing of Skyhawks. They placed it in a small compartment (Penue) designed to hold our radar altimeter. However, to install the camera the radar altimeter had to be removed. Since we required the radar altimeter for safety in night work, I had our technicians take out the camera and put back in the radar altimeter.

We took no combat pictures.

I was sitting in the ready room one day when a Commander from Commander Naval Air Force, Pacific staff came in and sat down beside me. He introduced himself as the "Pacific Fleet Camera Officer." He wanted to know why VA-153 was not taking any combat pictures. I told him, " We emphasize night attack, and we absolutely need the radar altimeter." He insisted, "the Navy needs combat pictures." I said, "I can't believe there is not a better place in the Skyhawk to place a camera." I sent for Chief Turgeon. I explained our problem, and asked Chief Turgeon if he could find a better place for a gun camera in the A4.

Within an hour, Chief Turgeon returned and invited us down to the hangar deck. He showed us there was in a void in the forward section of the middle bomb rack fairing where a camera could be installed. I ask Chief Turgeon to experiment with one of our airplanes on the hangar deck.

Within a day, Chief Turgeon had installed the 16 MM camera with a Plexiglas window and the necessary wiring in the center bomb rack void. It was nifty. Its only deficiency was the pilot had to turn on the camera by a separate switch, not the trigger for the guns. We were not allowed to modify existing aircraft wiring to make the camera run when the trigger was pulled.

Chief Turgeon decorated

Chief Turgeon drew up plans which we submitted to higher authority. His installation was approved and became the Fleet Standard camera installation for all Skyhawks, the Mopix. Here was a Navy Chief who out-thought and out-designed the entire Navy Bureau of Aeronautics!

I submitted a recommendation for a Navy Commendation and a cash award for Chief Turgeon. Both were approved.

Mobile   SA-2   SAM   Missile   Battery

Sam missile burst by Lt Steve Werlock on strike late 1966, Haiphong upper right

Toward the end of the month I was tired and impatient with hitting bridges. I was scheduled to lead a major strike on a bridge that we had knocked down several times before. There were significant flak batteries surrounding the target. The strike consisted of eight F-4 fighters for flak suppression, 16 A4 bombers, jammers and tankers. The North Vietnamese were moving in more Surface to Air Missiles (SAMs) every day.

During the briefing, Lieutenant Junior Grade John DeSantis, our Air Intelligence Officer, mentioned that there appeared to be several new surface-to-air missile sites being built along or near our route to the target. The typical surface-to-air missile site had five to seven circular earthen embankments built to protect each missile launcher with a center circular embankment protecting the guidance radars. Many times the North Vietnamese would build these sites, then move the missiles and radars in and out to other sites, at random. During the briefing, I asked John DeSantis, "Are these sites occupied?" He said, "I don't know, Skipper." This miffed me, I felt that intelligence should know whether missiles were in the site or not. So I said, "Well, we will fly by the missile sites, I'll look; if there are missiles there, that's what we will attack. The missiles are a better target than the bridge."

This provoked several fighter pilots in the back of the ready room, their comments indicated they weren't happy about going near the SAM sites. They obviously would prefer that I just stay away from the SAM sites completely. This just egged me on.

We launched, rendezvoused and proceeded toward the missile sites. As I approach the sites, I broke off with my wingman, we went ahead to look. I could see the sites were empty, so we proceeded on our route. This took us through an area of karst canyons in a place called "Quang Sui." Quang Sui was the area where our former Skipper, Commander Harry Thomas, had been shot down and killed the year before. It was a perfect place to hide gun positions, missile sites, military supplies and trucks. As we flew over Quang Sui I looked down and clearly saw, a mobile surface-to-air missile battery, a mobile SAM site! I called out the missile site to the flight and stated my intention to attack it.

SA-2 SAM Guideline Missile

The site was camouflaged and not easy to discern. The fighter leader, used to looking at the sky for MIGS, said he couldn't see the SAM site. Lieutenant Billy Byers, my wingman, confirmed my sighting, as did several other attack pilots.

I told the flight, "Bomb where I bomb," and rolled into my dive on the missile site.

At the same time, I realized that I better get pictures of the site. It was very unusual to find a mobile missile battery. This was the first for me in two years of fighting. The North Vietnamese moved these sites at night and kept them well hidden, under netting and other camouflage.

The second reason I needed a picture was political; the fighter leader couldn't see the target and I'm sure he would say it wasn't there. I asked Bill Byers, "Call the RA5C photo plane, tell him we need a picture of this missile site." Bill Byers switched channels to pass my request.

Bill reported back, the photo pilot refused to come. He said he was on a higher priority mission. I knew that a "Fleeting Target of Opportunity" which a SAM site was, was the highest priority, so I switched channels and ordered the RA5C pilot to take a picture of the Sam site. He again refused.

We bombed the mobile Sam site into a pile of rubble. All the time, Bill Byers and I both forgot. His aircraft had the first Chief Turgeon Blue Tail designed and built gun camera, the MOPIX! We could have taken our own movies!

When we landed back aboard, we knew we had just destroyed a surface-to-air missile site, we were sweaty, hot and upset that we had no photos of our feat. I knew the fighter pilots would claim there was no SAM site. We got out of our cockpits up on the bow and walked back down the deck together towards the debriefing room, I said something about that, "Five million dollar piece of crap," referring to the RA5C. My wingman, Bill Byers and Steve Macaleer picked up the theme and when we got into the debriefing room they started to "rag" the RA5C pilot and argue with the fighter pilots. As predicted, the fighter pilots said there was no SAM site. The RA5C pilot was a redheaded Lieutenant, who stayed on the other side of the debriefing room. I called him to come over to explain to me why he had disobeyed my order. Instead, he bolted out of the debriefing room to get his Commanding Officer, Commander Charlie Smith, who was notorious for having a very short fuse.

Charlie Smith and I met in the passageway. I explained my displeasure with his redheaded Lieutenant, who had disobeyed my direct order to get pictures of a top priority, "Fleeting Target of Opportunity," a SAM site. We came close to blows. Charlie gave me no satisfaction.

Next day, I was still mad about this incident. I was scheduled with my flight of four to bomb a bridge just to the south of Quang Sui. We all checked out Lica 35mm cameras and planned to return to Quang Sui after the bombing mission and take our own pictures of the Sam site. To hell with the RA5C! There had been no flak at Quang Sui the day before, right?

It was a bright and clear day, after bombing our bridge, I proceeded north at about 2000 feet to the area of the SAM site. I found the site and set up an easy 45 degree right bank at less at less than 300 knots with my flight in loose combat finger four formation. My section of two aircraft were high on my left and my wingmen below me on my right. I clearly saw the destroyed SAM site, raised my camera, centering the missile in my viewfinder.

I was about to snap the picture, when in the viewfinder, I saw red tongues of flame leap from mouths of seven 85 mm cannon placed near the destroyed SAM site.

'Boom, boom, boom, boom, boom, boom, boom!" A volley of black bursts instantly exploded with a roar all around us. The flak gunners had the perfect lead, a perfect shot, but no luck. We were right on top of the site and I knew that another volley would be fired in seconds. I waited for the tongues of flame from the seven 85 MM, then yelled, "Pull!" We pulled hard "Gs" together.

The next bursts missed us by several hundred yards. They fired three or four more times, but we spoiled their aim by pulling hard after each volley, until we danced out of their range.

I had broken one of my own, often preached, rules. "Never go back to the scene of the crime."

Pride.

It was only good fortune and the Grace of God, they didn't shoot down one or two of us. When we returned to the ship and debriefed, I apologized to the flight. They just laughed.

The next day, before briefing my flight, I entered the Integrated Intelligence Operations Center (IOIC) to get the latest intelligence photos. Prominently displayed, was a large photograph of our thoroughly destroyed mobile SAM battery, taken by an RA5C flown by ... Commander Charlie Smith.

CHAPTER EIGHTEEN

Final Battles

September-November 1966.

Tactical philosophy

My philosophy at this stage of the war was: stay aggressive, fight smart, minimize losses, maintain morale. We had a happy bunch of warriors. At sea, our bakers baked a cake for every possible occasion. I recall one for the Line Crew's hundredth tire change. It was apparent that the rules of engagement were not going to change significantly. For us it would remain a high risk,

Reyes, Harrington, Leue', O'Connell, Byers, Dienstl, Poore

low return war. I emphasized improving our night tactics and increasing use of the big Bullpup missile on bridges in the daytime, to minimize risks. We became the biggest Bullpup missile shooters in the fleet, by far.

To improve our truck kills at night we worked with a shore-based A3 pilot, Lieutenant Commander Ed Grady, who carried an early infrared scanner. Ed would fly, unarmed, over Route 1 in the black night and pass truck traffic information to us by message. We also worked with Army OV-10 pilots. The OV-10 had a side scanning radar. They flew off the coast tracking truck traffic which they passed to us. These innovations were developed through conversations started in the O-club.

We had an unusually strong group of combat leaders. Lieutenant Commanders Giuliani, O'Connell, Poore and Coleman were all tigers, as where our Lieutenants Herrington, Boardman, Byers, Kraus and Werlock. Demotivating them was my biggest task.

Danny O'Connell was a particular ball of fire, both on the beach and in combat. In maintaining our aircraft at their peak, he always seemed to be in a battle with the Air Boss, Commander Ken Enney, over aircraft spots, aircraft loading and maintenance. Throughout the cruise, Danny O'Connell remained an aggressive and effective day and night attack pilot. He destroyed many trucks on Route 1. Danny took great glee in it. We took turns on alternate nights burning trucks in Ha Tinh or sinking or harassing the "Cumquat Ferry." This large barge had gigantic outboard motors. Nightly, it carried trucks across a bridgeless inlet on

LCDR Bill Coakley

Route 1, inboard of Hon Me Island. This crossing was heavily defended with 37 MM. Only one fast pass was the rule. My last glimpse of the ferry, was on the deck, under the flares at 400 knots, the ferry was in a hard left turn with its outboards wide open, my gun pod was pouring a solid stream of 20MM. Did I hit it?

On the night of September 13, 1966, Danny was leading Bill Coakley attacking trucks north of the ferry. He had made his pass. Bill Coakley was slow following up, Danny called, "Bill are going to make your run or not? Coakley replied, "I'm trying Danny, I'm trying." Shortly, Danny observed a ball of fire, Bill Coalkey had crashed. Had he stalled, did he fly into a hill, was he shot down? We will never know what happened. Bill

Coakley was a outstanding officer, aviator and friend, my first loss as Skipper, he had been my courageous wingman in our wild PT caper just two days before. This was hard to take.

LTJG Harry Edwards

October 1966. The squadron received two young replacement pilots, Lieutenants Junior Grade Harry Edwards and Tom Newell. They were clean-cut, quiet Naval Academy graduates. I think they were a little overwhelmed with the high tempo of activity in our ready room. Lieutenant Commander Dick Coleman took both under his wing to teach them the rules of engagement (ROE), the squadron's standard operating procedures (SOP) and the thousand and one things they needed to know before they could fly combat missions with us. This orientation period lasted about one week.

Installation of the EKG before mission

On October 20, 1966, I was scheduled to lead a major strike on a bridge in Nam Dinh, a heavily defended city on Route 1 just 30 miles south of Hanoi. Lieutenant Junior Grade Edwards was scheduled to fly my right wing on this mission.

When I was the strike leader on major missions such as this, I gave two briefings. The first would be to the flight leaders of each squadron; this would take place two hours before the launch. The second briefing was given to VA-153 pilots in our ready room an hour before launch.

On this particular day, I had also volunteered to wear an EKG and recorder that would monitor my pulse and other vital signs during a combat mission. My old friend, Navy Flight Surgeon, Captain Doc Austin was aboard conducting research on combat stress.

Two and a half hours before the flight, I went to sick bay to get rigged up with sensors and recorder for this project. The weather for the flight was marginal, there had been many rain showers in the Gulf of Tonkin throughout the day. In briefing of the flight leaders, I paid particular attention to the flak. I emphasized the number of heavy 85 MM flak sites and went over my desired tactic of having the F-4 flak suppressors roll in first and hit the sites prior to the bombers commencing their dives.

We launched, rendezvoused and proceeded toward the beach. I kept the flight low flying at 200 feet over the water. Approaching the coastline I climbed to 4000 feet staying at that altitude flying at maximum speed to the target. At 4000 feet we were above most of the small arms. As I approached Nam Dinh, I noticed the river had overflowed and the area looked different from the maps due to the recent rain and low clouds. I turned left then back to the north to find the bridge. Once found, I kept the bridge on my right. I pulled my nose up zooming to 12,000 ready to commence my dive. I had briefed a roll-in to the right for a 45 degree dive, pulling out right heading toward the coast.

As I reached 12,000 feet, the flak suppressor leader announced, "I don't have the target." I kept my nose up arcing around the target to the right waiting for the F-4s flak suppressors to roll in. Finally, I couldn't wait, I rolled over into a very steep dive. I put my site on the target and called, "Pickle and pull!" My flight knew this meant, "We are steep, drop your bombs and pull, now!" I pulled about seven or eight "Gs" getting out of the dive, turned hard right then left, jinking, while looking for my bomb hit. I saw my bombs hit, then saw a ball of fire erupt beyond the target. I knew it was an aircraft. I had everyone check in; Harry Edwards was missing.

I sent my flight out over the water then went back and searched the target for any evidence of life. There was no chute, Harry Edwards had apparently gone straight in, just beyond the target. We returned to the ship and broke for landing, as I turned on final I said to myself, "My God! I've to got tell the squadron, I lost Harry Edwards on his first mission!"

When Doc Austin downloaded my vital signs it showed that I had a higher pulse rate approaching the ship than I did over the target. Based on the recorded data, it was widely reported in many circles, that carrier landings were more stressful than diving through flak in combat. I still hear this occasionally to this day. The data doesn't take into account my grief as I approached the ship.

We should never have flown Harry Edwards on that mission. Most likely he was shot down, we had no effective flak suppression on a target 30 miles SE of Hanoi with significant flak. However, my maneuvers on roll-in and the steep dive, routine to the old timers, may have been too much for Harry Edwards on my right wing. We should have scheduled him on an easy "piece of cake" two plane mission to start off. Life is not fair, this was Harry Edwards first mission, my three hundredth.

Missing in Action

On October 27, Lieutenant Bill Byers was scheduled as my wingman on a night reconnaissance mission. It was a black night with high overcast, with no moon. The ship was on the noon to midnight schedule. The briefing, launch and tanking all went in a routine fashion. After leaving the tanker as I was proceeding to the beach I noticed that my drop tank was not transferring. The emergency procedure for this malfunction was to pull the ram air turbine or RAT. The RAT was an emergency generator that popped out of the side of the aircraft. After dropping the RAT, my drop tank still would not transfer, but I elected to proceed with the mission. I planned to tank again later. We had a master electrical switch that had to be moved to drop ordinance. I was moving this master electrical switch from the RAT position back to internal, so I could drop flares as I was searching for trucks. I was talking to Bill Byers and the E2 surveillance aircraft and advised them that after the mission I would have to tank again, because my drop tank was not transferring.

Bill Byers and I had no luck in finding trucks, I told him I would make one more run and drop my ordinance on Route 1, then I would head back toward the ship, where I could tank before landing. In my dive, I lost all electrical power, lights, gauges, radio…. everything.

I knew Bill would be thinking the worst. I proceeded out over the water and tried repeatedly to get my generator back online, but had no luck. I orbited twice to see if I could pick up Bill Byers on his way back to the ship, but saw nothing. I was low on fuel, I had to make a decision fast on whether to try to find the ship 100 miles at sea over the black ocean with no radio and no navigation equipment, or try to find the Marine Airfield at Danang, Vietnam two hundred miles southeast. Easy choice. I knew I could find Danang, if I had enough fuel. I broke out my flashlight,　blew off my drop tank, climbed to an economical altitude and headed south.

I could not communicate with the tower to tell which runway was the duty runway so I orbited the field until I saw an aircraft takeoff. I quickly descended for landing.

I landed. The jolt shook lose a stuck relay, instantly restoring my electrical power, my lights came on and the radio started to work! I immediately called Danang tower, "This is Power

House One, I just landed, I am an A4C Skyhawk from VA-153, USS Constellation, they will be looking for me. Please inform them I am OK." I taxied in to transient parking to have the aircraft fueled. I hurried to PX to order a big hamburger. I had the Marines check over my aircraft, but they could find no problem.

Meanwhile, back in North Vietnam, LT Billy Byers, my faithful wingman, had alerted the ship I was missing. They launched an all out search for me.   I didn't return on the next recovery. The squadron prepared the Missing In Action messages.

I waited in Danang for over an hour before I received a message that I interpreted to mean, return to the ship for the 0200 recovery that night. I refueled and took off and flew out to Constellation at the appointed hour. I checked in shot my approach and landed with no problem.   Chief Turgeon, our maintenance chief, analyzed my fuel problem as a kinked drop tank hose and my electrical problem as water in a relay. I also found out the message that advised me to return was for 2 p.m. the next day. The ship had been secured from flight quarters when I returned.

Wives "Give—em Hell Honey " fly swatters

Captain Houser had ordered all aircraft pulled forward so I could land. This was a lot of work for the crew! The Captain was happy to have me back. I was happy to be back. I have a copy of a paragraph written in the squadron "Quotable quotes log," where the duty officer wrote:

LTJG Billy Byers: *"Skipper do you read me on guard? What is your position? Should I call for a rescue helo? Skipper, Skipper do you read me?"*

Meanwhile the Skipper, safe at Danang; "I'll have your biggest hamburger with everything on it."

This night mission with LT Billy Byers took place on October 27, 1966. For the next 12 days we continued to burn trucks at night, down bridges in the day with the Bullpup and continue our aggressive approach to the war. On 9 November 1966 I flew my last combat mission, a Bullpup strike on coastal guns.

VA-153 would come back many times in the next six years. I hoped to come back as Air Wing Commander. At this point, squadron morale was very high, we had every confidence our losses were not in vain. We believed we had done our part to ensure freedom for our South Vietnamese friends.

The price we paid. Air Wing Fifteen flying in the opening round of the Vietnam conflict from December 1964 to November 1966, from the decks of the USS Coral Sea and USS Constellation, sustained the following losses:

Embarked USS Coral Sea CVA-43:

7 February 1965: VA-155, LT E. A. Dickson, KIA.
11 February 1965 : VF-154, **LCDR R. H. Shumaker, POW.**
11 February 1965: A-4C, VA-153, **LT W. T. Majors, rescued.**
26 March 1965: F-8D, VF 154, **LT C. E. Wangeman Jr,** **rescued.**
29 March 1965: A-4E, VA-155, **CDR J. H. Harris, rescued.**
29 March 1965: F-8D, VF-154, **CDR W. N. Donnelly, rescued.**
29 March 1965: F-8D, VF-154, **LCDR K. E. Hume, KIA.**
7 April 1965: A-4C, VA-153, **LT W. M. Roark, KIA.**
9 April 1965: A-4C, VA-153, **LCDR C. H. McNeil, rescued.**
9 May 1965: F-8D, VF-154, **LT D. A. Kardell, KIA.**
25 June 1965: A-4C, VA-153, **CDR P. Mongilardi, KIA.**
15 July 1965: A-4C, VA-153, **LT A. J. Bennett, rescued.**
12 August 1965: A-4E, VA-155, **LT W. T. Fidelibus, recovered.**
13 August 1965: A-1H, VA-165, **LT R. Hyland, rescued.**
13 August 1965: RF-8A, VFP-63, **LT P. A. Manning,**

recovered.
13 August 1965: A-4C, VA-153, **CDR H E Thomas, KIA.**
4 September 1965: A-1H, VA-165, **LTJG E B Shaw, KIA.**
7 September 1965: RF-8A,VFP-63, **LTJG C B Goodwin, MIA.**
10 September 1965: A-4E, VA-155, **LCDR W B Rivers, POW.**
11 October 1965: A-4E,VA-155, **LCDR P M Moore, rescued.**
14 October 1965: F-8D,VF-154, **LT J A Terhune, rescued.**

Embarked USS Constellation CVA-64:

23 June 1966: F-4B **both crewmembers KIA.**

25 June 1966: A-6A, VA-65, **LT R. M. Weber, recovered,   and LTJG C. W. Marik, KIA.**
27 June 1966: A-4E, VA-155, **LCDR G. A. Smith, KIA.**
1 July 1966: A-4E VA-155, **CDR Chuck H. Peters, KIA.**
4 July 1966: A-4E VA-155, **LT N. E. Holben, rescued.**

11 July 1966: A-4C, VA-153, **LCDR G. H. Wilkins, KIA.**
29 July 1966: A4E, VA-155, **LTJG V. K. Cameron, KIA.**

10 August 1966: A-4E, VA-155, **LCDR J. Heuriques, KIA.**
19 August 1966: RA-5C, **LCDR J. K. Thompson and LTJG G. L. Parten, both rescued.**
27 August 1966: A-6A, VA-65, **LCDR J. H. Fellowes and LTJG G. T. Coker, both POW.**
13 September 1966: A-4C, VA-153, **LCDR Bill Coakley, KIA.**

19 September 1966: F-4B, VF-151, **both crewmembers KIA.**
20 October 1966: A-4C, VA-153, **LTJG Harry S. Edwards, KIA.**
22 October 1966: F-4B, VF-161, **LCDR E. P. McBride, KIA, and LTJG E. U. Turner, rescued.**
22 October 1966: RA-5C, RVAH-6, **LCDR T. C. Kolstad and LTJG W. B. Klenert, both KIA.**

Those we lost were our family and best friends. They were all volunteers, skilled, the best and brightest with degrees and knowledge of the world. They all believed in the fight for free Vietnam.

CHAPTER NINETEEN

Home Again

December 2, 1966. My logbook shows the squadron launched from USS Constellation off the coast of California and flew to NAS Lemoore at about noon. It was a joyous homecoming. Jane had done an amazing job keeping up the morale of the squadron wives and taking care of our growing

VA-153 personnel arrive home December 2, 1966

Becky, Cathy, Emily, Speckie, Papa, Krista, Paul, Debbie, Lemoore

family. The family and squadron enjoyed November and December getting together for skiing trips and trips to Yosemite.

Eric, the cute little black lab puppy that I bought for Paul, was now a beautiful, uncontrollable, large black lab. The entire neighborhood had bad things to say about him. Jane had gotten nasty calls many nights while I was gone, complaining. It was not the dog's fault, he needed a strong hand and I was gone. We gave Eric to a good home, and inherited a beautiful, shy, German Shorthaired Pointer from a First-Class Machinist Mate in VA-153. We named him, "Speckie." The family

Blue Tail A4E

instantly loved Speckie, and he loved us. He would be a part of the Leue's for many years.

In January, the squadron received the newer model Skyhawk, the A4E. This model Skyhawk had a more powerful Pratt Whitney engine and two more weapons stations. We commenced training in earnest with this new model aircraft. Once again, the squadron geared up for the short turn-around to deploy again in the middle of 1967. Commander Tom Woolcock proved to be strong and steady in combat, he would take over the squadron sometime in the spring.

Again, several of our key officers were transferred to other commands. Lieutenant Commander Charlie Earnest came aboard and was assigned Maintenance Officer. Charlie was a unique individual that rode motorcycles and had a machine shop that he used to produce scale model steam engines. I would later serve with Charlie in my Pentagon tour. His wife, Mina, was a genuine, lovable, character. She and Jane became fast friends. Charlie would later lead his own A6A squadron in Vietnam and die there.

In April, I received orders to Staff, Commander Naval Air Forces, ComNavAirPac, Pacific in San Diego. We put the house up for sale and prepared to move to San Diego.

Change of Command

In June 1967, I was relieved of Command of Light Attack Squadron by Commander Tom Woolcock. This was a festive day with Jane and the children, my extended family, including my mother, sister Dolly and her husband Speas Anderson.

Jane received a beautiful handmade memento signed by all the squadron wives. It was covered by our squadron patch and expressed their love and appreciation for all she had done to help, guide and console them for two years.

My remarks centered on the sacrifice, professionalism and performance of the squadron pilots and enlisted personnel. I emphasized the fact we had lost aircraft and pilots to enemy fire,

June 1967 VA-153 Change of Command scenes; Krista, Jane and Others

but none to accidents. I also paid tribute to our fallen comrades, the squadron wives and families, who had supported us so strongly. I wished the squadron well as it returned to combat.

I read my orders. After the celebration we departed for our new duty station in San Diego.

CHAPTER TWENTY

My heroes, Navy Light Attack Squadron 153, USS Constellation CVA-64 , 1966

Reflections

Vietnam Irony

1967. Departing the Blue Tails I had no idea what the final outcome of the conflict in Vietnam might be. No one did. I was emotionally invested in the Vietnamese cause. Could I return to the battle as Air Wing Commander? My orders were to the staff of the Commander-In-Chief Naval Air Forces, Pacific Fleet in San Diego.

1968. We purchased a new home in the Lake Murray area of San Diego. The family was thriving. I served as the Pacific Fleet Attack Training Officer directing the training and equipping of Naval light attack squadrons deploying to Vietnam. A great job, but I read dispatch after dispatch announcing the loss of close friends in Vietnam; Commander Larry Dion, Lieutenant Commander Carol Crane, Lieutenant Commander Stan Olmstead, Commander Fred

Leue's San Diego 1968

Whittemore, Commander Homer Smith. Commander Woolcock, who relieved me as CO of VA-153 is shot by a SA-2 missile and rescued, Lieutenant Mike Allard is shot down and killed. Eleven of the Blue Tails twelve aircraft have been shot down in this war so far.

January 1968. The Tet Offensive. In Hue' City, the old capital, the North Vietnamese, believing they had won the war, round up the mayor, all the city fathers, the police, the teachers and any who are tainted by association with the Americans. They are shot in the back of the head and bulldozed into a pit, ala Stalin. Two weeks later, the Marines fight their way back into Hue, they find thousands of bound and gagged bodies. This is a precursor of what will happen to the South Vietnamese if Ho Chi Minh wins. (Did the press keep this story from the American people for a reason?)

May 13, 1968 We celebrate the biggest event of the year. Jane brings forth Barbara (Bonnie) our seventh, with apparent ease.

Jane and Bonnie, May 1968

November 1968. Richard Nixon is elected president.

1969. Ho Chi Minh dies. I am selected Air Wing Commander. I am told I cannot return to combat. I go instead to Carrier Air Wing Seven on USS

Independence, home port, Norfolk, Virginia.

On a visit to family in Hornell, New York I am approached by a local newspaper reporter for an interview about my Vietnam combat experience. This interview turns into a shouting match. The reporter insists I accept his views of the Vietnam conflict, acquired I imagine, from the left-wing diatribes of the NY Times. We narrowly avoided a physical confrontation. Of course, there was no article published containing my views of the war. I can't imagine this sort of thing taking place when Joe Stalin was our ally in World War II.

1970. The Vietnam conflict drags on with a series of bombing halts and violent attacks. Opposition to the war in our universities reaches a fever pitch. Egged on by the press and campus leftists, the NROTC at CAL Berkeley and the Pentagon are bombed by radicals. It is difficult to watch from afar.

In July, I record my last carrier landing on USS Independence in an F4J in the Bay of Naples, Mediterranean Sea. I receive orders as Assistant for Tactical Air Planning, OP- 50, in the Pentagon.

CDR Dave Leue', CAG-7 last launch in VF-102 F4J July 15,1970

I again work with Commander Charlie Ernest now in the office of the Secretary of Defense. Charlie had been VA 153's maintenance officer in 1967. He had survived the 1967-68 combat cruise on USS Coral Sea. Charlie screens for in an A6A squadron command and begins commuting to Virginia Beach from Washington DC for A6A training. Driving his old Dodge van he comes upon burning railroad ties in the middle of the freeway. The railroad ties were placed there by Vietnam war protesters. Charlie attacks the barricades and the protesters with his van. He told me he scattered both, chasing them through the fields, then drove happily on his way with a thoroughly dented van.

May 1972. In an attempt to bring the North Vietnamese to the negotiating table, President Nixon mines Haiphong harbor in Operation Linebacker. In 1965, mining was rejected by President Johnson when proposed by General Maxwell Taylor. Nixon's action proves more effective in stopping Soviet war supplies than years of bombing by "Rolling Thunder."

March 1972. I serve as Commanding Officer USS Canisteo, AO-99, a 650 foot armed replenishment ship in the Mediterranean Sea.

USS Canisteo AO-99

December 18, 1972. President Nixon authorizes Linebacker II. He re-mines Haiphong harbor and bombs military targets around Hanoi using Air Force B-52's with Navy, Air Force and Marine tactical air. This dramatic action brings the North Vietnamese to the negotiating table. (An excellent history of these events is given in *To Hanoi and Back* by Wayne Thompson)

We have armed and trained the South Vietnamese Army and

Air Force. They need our continuing materiel and air support to survive.

In exchange for our prisoners in the Hanoi Hilton, we promise to remove American forces from South Vietnam and remove the mines from Haiphong harbor. (My prediction comes true).

The North Vietnamese promise not to move anymore forces into South Vietnam. President Nixon assures South Vietnamese President Thieu, that if the North Vietnamese came back, we will come back.

1973. In direct defiance of the President's pledge to President Thieu, progressives in our Congress pass the Second Supplemental Appropriations Act For Fiscal Year 1973. *This Act prohibits use of any funds to: "Support directly or indirectly combat activities in or over Cambodia, Laos, North Vietnam or South Vietnam, or off the shores of Cambodia, Laos, North Vietnam and South Vietnam."*

This act of Congress assures victory to our communist enemy, North Vietnam, and death for our allies in South Vietnam, Laos and Cambodia.

1973-1974. Without our air or material support, South Vietnam fights on alone, while the Soviet Union massively increases the supplies of tanks and heavy artillery to the North Vietnamese.

RADM Coogan

RADM Small

October 1974. I serve as Chief of Staff, Carrier Group Three for RADM Robert Coogan and RADM William Small.

1975. Saigon falls. This is the high water mark for Communism. The world wide and American Left celebrate.

Millions of Vietnamese flee the wonders of communism

1976. Millions of South Vietnamese are thrown into retraining camps or killed outright. The massive flow of "Boat People" from 1975 – 1980, is dramatic evidence of the holocaust. The U.S. Press looks the other way.

1976-1977. I serve as Chief of Staff, Light Attack Wing

Twenty Fifth Anniversary

Professor Dave Leue'

Pacific at NAS Lemoore, California then retire from military duty.

1985-1990. As a professor at Fresno State University several Vietnamese and Laotian students in my classes relate stories of capture, incarceration, abuse, torture, and becoming "Boat People."

1991. The Soviet Union collapses. Vietnam pleads for U.S. trade and aid after support from the Soviet Union is lost.

Naval Air.

Naval Air's involvement in Vietnam spanned nine years, from January 1964 to June 1973. It paid a heavy price. The Navy lost 854 aircraft, 538 to combat and 316 operationally. In that era, flying from aircraft carriers in all weather, night and day, was almost as deadly as combat.

Most combat losses, 55%, were to antiaircraft artillery and automatic weapons. Surface-To-Air missiles accounted for 15%, another 37% were from unknown causes. Our own ordinance (bomb blast & premature detonation) accounted for more losses (3%) than from enemy Migs (2%).

"Rolling Thunder'" the Navy and Air Force piecemeal air attack on the heavily defended transportation system, was a failure. Had President Johnson followed the JCS advice in 1965 to mine Haiphong harbor, with the support of our press and élites, ala WWII, we may have a free, thriving and productive South Vietnam today.

Why did we fight?

The battle for the free people of Vietnam arose from the philosophical, political and military power of the Soviet Union. In my first volume, "Korean Combat, The Four Freedoms

Betrayed," it was shown that both the Korean and Vietnamese wars flowed directly from Franklin Delano Roosevelt's arming of Joe Stalin and the Soviets. Roosevelt betrayed his pledge given in his "Four Freedoms" speech "to fight those dictators." (See Appendix A). If FDR had fought and defeated Stalin and the Soviet Union, with Hitler, in WWII as he pledged, there would have been no "Cold War," Korean War or Vietnamese Wars.

In reading Richard Nixon's *Memoirs*, and Henry Kissinger's, *Years of Upheaval*, I was struck by the realization that LBJ's Nixon's and Kissinger's greatest challenge in trying to gain a meaningful peace in Vietnam and explain US policy and objectives to the American people, was our own hostile media and universities that supported the socialist philosophies of our opponents! Our media's support of our enemies was a key factor in the war's outcome.

Summing Up

Our sacrifices in Vietnam accelerated the demise of the Soviet Union. The battle against Communism was just another battle in the continuing quest for the free society our founders envisioned. It continues today in our own nation.

Our founders crafted the Constitution of the United States. This revolutionary document for the first time set forth an elected government with powers granted by the Almighty, shared by the judicial, legislative and executive branches, supported by a free-market economy.

Our founders risked all to fight the oppression of Kings and Queens. In my time, national and international socialism replaced kings and queens as oppressors. They called themselves progressives.

Witness recent history:

Hitler, Stalin, Khrushchev, Mao, Kim Ill Son, Castro, Pol Pot, Ho Chi Minh and lesser depots.

Did they bring the world progress?

Hardly. These socialist regimes supported by "progressives" gave their people gulags, graves and abject poverty. Why should we elect leaders and support parties that emulate them?

You may call me "Conservative." I prefer, "Revolutionary."

Support the Constitution, continue the quest for "The Four Freedoms" throughout the world.

David E. Jene

Vietnam at War: The History 1946 – 1975 — Philip B. Davidson

On Yankee Station: The Air War in Vietnam— Commander John B. Nichols USN (Ret)

Healing from a War: Trauma and Transformation after Vietnam — Arthor Egendorf

Dateline: Vietnam —Jim G. Lucas

The Cold War: A Military History —Ambrose, Carr, Fleming, Victor Davis Hanson, etc.

The Press and the Cold War— James Aronson

Vietnam: The Naval Story— Frank Uhlig Jr.

Cheating Death: Combat Air Rescues in Vietnam And Laos— George J. Merritt

Our Vietnam: The War 1954 -1975—A. J. Langguth

No Peace No Honor—Larry Berman

Shattered Peace—Daniel Yergin

In the Jaws of History —Bui Diem with David Chanoff

Dishonored Glory: Colonel Bo's Vietnam War Journal —Heath Bottomly

In Love and War— Jim and Sybil Stockdale

Years of Upheaval—Henry Kissinger

Memoirs—Richard Nixon

Vietnam: A History—Stanley Karnow

On Yankee Station—Commander John B. Nichols USN (Ret)

Peace with Honor?—Stuart A. Herrington

Survivors: Vietnam POWs Tell Their Stories—Zalin Grant

To Hanoi and Back—Wayne Thompson

A Bright and Shining Lie—Neil Sheehan

After the War Was Over—Hanoi and Saigon   Neil Sheehan

The Heart of a Man—Frank Elkins

Faith of My Fathers—John McCain

Here Is Your Enemy—James Cameron's Complete Report From North Vietnam

Prisoner of War: Six Years in Hanoi—John M. McGrath

Our Vietnam Nightmare—Marguerite Higgins

Stalking the Viet Cong—Stuart A. Herrington

March to Calumny—Albert D. Biderman

The Captives of Korea—William L. White

Nixon off the Record —Monica Crowley

Alpha Strike Vietnam: The Navy's air war 1964 to 1973   Jeffrey L. Levinson

Fox Two: the story of America's First Ace in Vietnam—Randy Cunningham with Jeff Ethell

Before Honor —Eugène B. McDaniel

The State of the Union Speech was given by FDR January 6, 1941. At this time Hitler and Stalin were allies. Together these two dictators had attacked Poland in September 1939. Together they had overrun Europe. Stalin had already killed millions and Hitler was about to do the same.

Mr. President, Mr. Speaker, Members of the Seventy-seventh Congress:

I address you, the Members of the Seventy-seventh Congress, at a moment unprecedented in the history of the Union. I use the word "unprecedented," because at no previous time has American security been as seriously threatened from without as it is today.

Since the permanent formation of our Government under the Constitution, in 1789, most of the periods of crisis in our history have related to our domestic affairs. Fortunately, only one of these the four-year War between the States ever threatened our national unity. Today, thank God, one hundred and thirty million Americans, in forty-eight States, have forgotten points of the compass in our national unity.

It is true that prior to 1914 the United States often had been disturbed by events in other Continents. We had even engaged in two wars with European nations and in a number of undeclared wars in the West Indies, in the Mediterranean and in the Pacific for the maintenance of American rights and for the principles of peaceful commerce. But in no case had a serious threat been raised against our national safety or our continued independence.

What I seek to convey is the historic truth that the United States as a nation has at all times maintained clear, definite opposition, to any attempt to lock us in behind an ancient Chinese wall while the procession of civilization went past. Today, thinking of our children and of their children, we oppose enforced isolation for ourselves or for any other part of the Americas.

That determination of ours, extending over all these years, was proved, for example, during the quarter century of wars following the French Revolution.

While the Napoleonic struggles did threaten interests of the United States because of the French foothold in the West Indies and in Louisiana, and while we engaged in the War of 1812 to vindicate our right to peaceful trade, it is nevertheless clear that neither France nor Great Britain, nor any other nation, was aiming at domination of the whole world.

In like fashion from 1815 to 1914 ninety-nine years no single war in Europe or in Asia constituted a real threat against our future or against the future of any other American nation.

Except in the Maximilian interlude in Mexico, no foreign power sought to establish itself in this Hemisphere; and the strength of the British fleet in the Atlantic has been a friendly strength. It is still a friendly strength.

Even when the World War broke out in 1914, it seemed to contain only small threat of danger to our own American future. But, as time went on, the American people began to visualize what the downfall of democratic nations might mean to our own democracy.

We need not overemphasize imperfections in the Peace of Versailles. We need not harp on failure of the democracies to deal with problems of world reconstruction. We should remember that the Peace of 1919 was far less unjust than the kind of "pacification" which began even before Munich, and which is being carried on under the new order of tyranny that seeks to spread over every continent today. The American people have unalterably set their faces against that tyranny.

Every realist knows that the democratic way of life is at this moment being' directly assailed in every part of the world assailed either by arms, or by secret spreading of poisonous propaganda by those who seek to destroy unity and promote discord in nations that are still at peace.

During sixteen long months this assault has blotted out the whole pattern of democratic life in an appalling number of independent nations, great and small. The assailants are still on the march, threatening other nations, great and small.

Therefore, as your President, performing my constitutional duty to "give to the Congress information of the state of the Union," I find it, unhappily, necessary to report that the future and the safety of our country and of our democracy are overwhelmingly involved in events far beyond our borders.

Armed defense of democratic existence is now being gallantly waged in four continents. If that defense fails, all the population and all the resources of Europe, Asia, Africa and Australasia will be dominated by the conquerors. Let us remember that the total of those populations and their resources in those four continents greatly exceeds the sum total of the population and the resources of the whole of the Western Hemisphere-many times over.

In times like these it is immature and incidentally, untrue for anybody to brag that an unprepared America, single-handed, and with one hand tied behind its back, can hold off the whole world.

No realistic American can expect from a dictator's peace international generosity, or return of true independence, or world disarmament, or freedom of expression, or freedom of religion -or even good business.

Such a peace would bring no security for us or for our neighbors. "Those, who would give up essential liberty to purchase a little temporary safety, deserve neither liberty nor safety."

As a nation, we may take pride in the fact that we are softhearted; but we cannot afford to be soft-headed.

We must always be wary of those who with sounding brass and a tinkling cymbal preach the "ism" of appeasement.

We must especially beware of that small group of selfish men who would clip the wings of the American eagle in order to feather their own nests.

I have recently pointed out how quickly the tempo of modern warfare could bring into our very midst the physical attack which we must eventually expect if the dictator nations win this war.

There is much loose talk of our immunity from immediate and direct invasion from across the seas. Obviously, as long as the British Navy retains its power, no such danger exists. Even if there were no British Navy, it is not probable that any enemy would be stupid enough to attack us by landing troops in the United States from across thousands of miles of ocean, until it had acquired strategic bases from which to operate.

But we learn much from the lessons of the past years in Europe-particularly the lesson of Norway, whose essential seaports were captured by treachery and surprise built up over a series of years.

The first phase of the invasion of this Hemisphere would not be the landing of regular troops. The necessary strategic points would be occupied by secret agents and their dupes-and great numbers of them are already here, and in Latin America.

As long as the aggressor nations maintain the offensive, they-not we will choose the time and the place and the method of their attack.

That is why the future of all the American Republics is today in serious danger.

That is why this Annual Message to the Congress is unique in our history.

That is why every member of the Executive Branch of the Government and every member of the Congress faces great responsibility and great accountability.

The need of the moment is that our actions and our policy should be devoted primarily-almost exclusively to meeting this foreign peril. For all our domestic problems are now a part of the great emergency.

Just as our national policy in internal affairs has been based upon a decent respect for the rights and the dignity of all our fellow men within our gates, so our national policy in foreign affairs has been based on a decent respect for the rights and dignity of all nations, large and small. And the justice of morality must and will win in the end.

Our national policy is this:

First, by an impressive expression of the public will and without regard to partisanship, we are committed to all-inclusive national defense.

Second, by an impressive expression of the public will and without regard to partisanship, we are committed to full support of all those resolute peoples, everywhere, who are resisting aggression and are thereby keeping war away from our Hemisphere. By this support, we express our determination that the democratic cause shall prevail; and we strengthen the defense and the security of our own nation.

Third, by an impressive expression of the public will and without regard to partisanship, we are committed to the proposition that principles of morality and considerations for our own security will never permit us to acquiesce in a peace dictated by aggressors and sponsored by appeasers. We know that enduring peace cannot be bought at the cost of other people's freedom.

In the recent national election there was no substantial difference between the two great parties in respect to that national policy. No issue was fought out on this line before the American electorate. Today it is abundantly evident that American citizens everywhere are demanding and supporting speedy and complete action in recognition of obvious danger.

Therefore, the immediate need is a swift and driving increase in our armament production.

Leaders of industry and labor have responded to our summons. Goals of speed have been set. In some cases these goals are being reached ahead of time; in some cases we are on schedule; in other cases there are slight but not serious delays; and in some cases and I am sorry to say very important cases we are all concerned by the slowness of the accomplishment of our plans.

The Army and Navy, however, have made substantial progress during the past year. Actual experience is improving and speeding up our methods of production with every passing day. And today's best is not good enough for tomorrow.

I am not satisfied with the progress thus far made. The men in charge of the program represent the best in training, in ability, and in patriotism. They are not satisfied with the progress thus far made. None of us will be satisfied until the job is done.

No matter whether the original goal was set too high or too low, our objective is quicker and better results. To give you two illustrations:

We are behind schedule in turning out finished airplanes; we are working day and night to solve the innumerable problems and to catch up.

We are ahead of schedule in building warships but we are working to get even further ahead of that schedule.

To change a whole nation from a basis of peacetime production of implements of peace to a basis of wartime production of implements of war is no small task. And the greatest difficulty comes at the beginning of the program, when new tools, new plant facilities, new assembly lines, and new ship ways must first be constructed before the actual materiel begins to flow steadily and speedily from them.

The Congress, of course, must rightly keep itself informed at all times of the progress of the program. However, there is certain information, as the Congress itself will readily recognize, which, in the interests of our own security and those of the nations that we are supporting, must of needs be kept in confidence.

New circumstances are constantly begetting new needs for our safety. I shall ask this Congress for greatly increased new appropriations and authorizations to carry on what we have begun.

I also ask this Congress for authority and for funds sufficient to manufacture additional munitions and war supplies of many kinds, to be turned over to those nations which are now in actual war with aggressor nations.

Our most useful and immediate role is to act as an arsenal for them as well as for ourselves. They do not need man power, but they do need billions of dollars' worth of the weapons of defense.

The time is near when they will not be able to pay for them all in ready cash. We cannot, and we will not, tell them that they must surrender, merely because of present inability to pay for the weapons which we know they must have.

I do not recommend that we make them a loan of dollars with which to pay for these weapons loan to be repaid in dollars.

I recommend that we make it possible for those nations to continue to obtain war materials in the United States, fitting their orders into our own program. Nearly all their materiel would, if the time ever came, be useful for our own defense.

Taking counsel of expert military and naval authorities, considering what is best for our own security, we are free to decide how much should be kept here and how much should be sent abroad to our friends who by their determined and heroic resistance are giving us time in which to make ready our own defense.

For what we send abroad, we shall be repaid within a reasonable time following the close of hostilities, in similar materials, or, at our option, in other goods of many kinds, which they can produce and which we need.

Let us say to the democracies: "We Americans are vitally concerned in your defense of freedom. We are putting forth our energies, our resources and our organizing powers to give you the strength to regain and maintain a free world. We shall send you, in ever-increasing numbers, ships, planes, tanks, guns. This is our purpose and our pledge."

In fulfillment of this purpose we will not be intimidated by the threats of dictators that they will regard as a breach of international law or as an act of war our aid to the democracies which dare to resist their aggression. Such aid is not an act of war, even if a dictator should unilaterally proclaim it so to be.

When the dictators, if the dictators, are ready to make war upon us, they will not wait for an act of war on our part. They did not wait for Norway or Belgium or the Netherlands to commit an act of war.

Their only interest is in a new one-way international law, which lacks mutuality in its observance, and, therefore, becomes an instrument of oppression.

The happiness of future generations of Americans may well depend upon how effective and how immediate we can make our aid felt. No one can tell the exact character of the emergency situations that we may be called upon to meet. The Nation's hands must not be tied when the Nation's life is in danger.

We must all prepare to make the sacrifices that the emergency-almost as serious as war itself demands. Whatever stands in the way of speed and efficiency in defense preparations must give way to the national need.

A free nation has the right to expect full cooperation from all groups. A free nation has the right to look to the leaders of business, of labor, and of agriculture to take the lead in stimulating effort, not among other groups but within their own groups.

The best way of dealing with the few slackers or trouble makers in our midst is, first, to shame them by patriotic example, and, if that fails, to use the sovereignty of Government to save Government.

As men do not live by bread alone, they do not fight by armaments alone. Those who man our defenses, and those behind them who build our defenses, must have the stamina and the courage which come from unshakable belief in the manner of life which they are defending. The mighty action that we are calling for cannot be based on a disregard of all things worth fighting for.

The Nation takes great satisfaction and much strength from the things which have been done to make its people conscious of their individual stake in the preservation of democratic life in America. Those things have toughened the fiber of our people, have renewed their faith and strengthened their devotion to the institutions we make ready to protect.

Certainly this is no time for any of us to stop thinking about the social and economic problems which are the root cause of the social revolution which is today a supreme factor in the world.

For there is nothing mysterious about the foundations of a healthy and strong democracy. The basic things expected by our people of their political and economic systems are simple. They are:

Equality of opportunity for youth and for others.
Jobs for those who can work.
Security for those who need it.
The ending of special privilege for the few.
The preservation of civil liberties for all.

The enjoyment of the fruits of scientific progress in a wider and constantly rising standard of living.

These are the simple, basic things that must never be lost sight of in the turmoil and unbelievable complexity of our modern world. The inner and abiding strength of our economic and political systems is dependent upon the degree to which they fulfill these expectations.

Many subjects connected with our social economy call for immediate improvement. As examples:

We should bring more citizens under the coverage of old-age pensions and unemployment insurance.

We should widen the opportunities for adequate medical care.

We should plan a better system by which persons deserving or needing gainful employment may obtain it.

I have called for personal sacrifice. I am assured of the willingness of almost all Americans to respond to that call.

A part of the sacrifice means the payment of more money in taxes. In my Budget Message I shall recommend that a greater portion of this great defense program be paid for from taxation than we are paying today. No person should try, or be allowed, to get rich out of this program; and the principle of tax payments in accordance with ability to pay should be constantly before our eyes to guide our legislation.

If the Congress maintains these principles, the voters, putting patriotism ahead of pocketbooks, will give you their applause.

In the future days, which we seek to make secure, we look forward to a world founded upon four essential human freedoms.

The first is freedom of speech and expression everywhere in the world.

The second is freedom of every person to worship God in his own way everywhere in the world.

The third is freedom from want which, translated into world terms, means economic understandings which will secure to every nation a healthy peacetime life for its inhabitants-everywhere in the world.

The fourth is freedom from fear which, translated into world terms, means a world-wide reduction of armaments to such a point and in such a thorough fashion that no nation will be in a position to commit an act of physical aggression against any neighbor anywhere in the world.

That is no vision of a distant millennium. It is a definite basis for a kind of world attainable in our own time and generation. That kind of world is the very antithesis of the so-called new order of tyranny which the dictators seek to create with the crash of a bomb.

To that new order we oppose the greater conception the moral order. A good society is able to face schemes of world domination and foreign revolutions alike without fear.

Since the beginning of our American history, we have been engaged in change in a perpetual peaceful revolution a revolution which goes on steadily, quietly adjusting itself to changing conditions without the concentration camp or the quick-lime in the ditch. The world order which we seek is the cooperation of free countries, working together in a friendly, civilized society.

This nation has placed its destiny in the hands and heads and hearts of its millions of free men and women; and its faith in freedom under the guidance of God. Freedom means the supremacy of human rights everywhere. Our support goes to those who struggle to gain those rights or keep them. Our strength is our unity of purpose. To that high concept there can be no end save victory.

Made in the USA
Lexington, KY
03 January 2014